THE BUS
BIRTH
BLUEPRINT

How-to Establish a Nonprofit Business Incubator
(not just a Real Estate Operation!)
that Nurtures Entrepreneurs and Grows
Thriving Start-up Ventures

SHANNON CORMIER WILLIAMS, PH.D.

The Business Birthing Blueprint: How to Establish a Nonprofit Business Incubator (*not* just a Real Estate Operation!) that Nurtures Entrepreneurs and Grows Thriving Start-up Ventures

For permissions, please address correspondence to:
Shannon Williams P.O. Box 958285, Duluth, GA 30095.
www.businessbirthingblueprint.com

Second Edition
ISBN: 978-0-9991996-1-9

DEDICATION

To Dr. Dana Carson

&

Dr. John Sibley Butler

Two of the greatest powerhouse mentors a person could ever
hope to have in life.

TABLE OF CONTENTS

INTRODUCTION

The Birth of an Entrepreneurial Evangelist

Some exposures and experiences in life can be so impactful that they resonate with everything inside of us and some kind of way, manage to set all of our insides *afire*! This is exactly what I can recall experiencing when I was just a little southern girl with big dreams in Houston, Texas, with a thirst for life and a voracious appetite for knowledge. I lived within walking distance of my most beloved and favorite aunt, Colita. Aunt Colita was not only my favorite because she had an affinity for high fashion, she was also ambitious before it became popular for women to be so, blatantly outspoken in such a way that one never had to wonder what was on her mind, the life of the party, hilarious, and overflowing with kindness, love and generosity. All of those things helped to build the case for why she was easily one of my favorite relatives on earth. However, what sealed the deal and placed Aunt Colita in my number one spot was that she was an entrepreneur – a girl boss! Imagine me, a young girl, walking to my Aunt's house in Houston's pre-gentrified Third Ward neighborhood, a looming two-story red-brick house that sat prominently perched on a corner lot and served as a source of pride for everyone in the neighborhood. I would walk into the immense house, which felt to me like a mansion at the time, and behold the rich commercial-grade tapestries, modern kitchen, fine wooden furniture (no particleboard here!), exquisite crystal, and fine art that decorated every inch of the abode.

As soon as she saw me walk through the screen door (necessary even on the palatial dwelling because this was Houston, where mosquitoes grow large enough to carry small children away), my Aunt Colita would scoop me up in her arms with a loud, southern "Oooooo! Look who's here! It's my *niece*! Come here, baby, and give Aunt Colita a hug!" After a big hug, she would begin gathering her things; her niece was here, so we had somewhere to go. Preparing for our departure, she would chatter non-stop: "Ooooo, your Aunt Colita has been so busy! I hit three estate sales this week and got some new stuff in my shop. *Nice* stuff, because you know, Aunt Colita doesn't buy *anything* cheap. When you get something, you make *sure* it's quality! You hear me? Quality! Yesssss!" By the way, yes, Aunt Colita always spoke of herself in the third person, another trait that made her unusual and so darn captivating!

After shutting everything down in the house and grabbing her keys, my aunt would look at me and ask, "You ready?" I would nod yes and head for the screen door. We had somewhere to go! A short descent down the cement steps that were right outside the screen door led to the front yard, about eight paces after that led toward the neighborhood side street, and upon crossing the street, we were in Aunt Colita's territory: the whole darn block was hers! I felt such an overwhelming sense of admiration, and my heart burst with pride every time I beheld her business ventures that sat right across the street from her house. She owned all of the property and the real estate on the block: the corner store, the resale shop, the barber shop, the row houses for rent... everything! When I walked on that territory, I was walking with the boss lady, who just happened to be my aunt! She did not take orders, she gave them. She did not pay money, she collected it. She did not yield to others, others yielded to her. She would take me into each one of her businesses and have everyone greet me. "Heyyy, everybody! How are you all doing today? Say hello to my niece. This is Shannon!"

Everyone would greet me, partly out of the spirit of southern hospitality which calls for offering a sincere and polite welcome to anyone who steps into a room, and partly – probably mostly – out of obligation, because Mrs. Gillespie had instructed them to do so. Mrs.

Colita Gillespie's name was well recognized; she held the respect of everyone in the neighborhood. Even then, as a little girl, I recognized that because of who she was, people *wanted* her to like them. People *wanted* to shake her hand. People *wanted* to be in her good graces, rub shoulders with her, and be invited to one of her famous amazing parties. I also realized that the lofty level of respect and regard they held for her was neither because of her wonderful personality, nor because of her willingness to share a kind word or a hot meal with anyone in need. It was not because she donned several fur coats in a climate that made the opportunity to wear them as infrequent as the appearance of Haley's comet or because of her nice big, lavish house and its fine furnishings. Instead, her prominence was directly attributable to her position of being an owner. A boss. An entrepreneur.

After making the rounds with me at her side, my Aunt Colita would take me into her corner store. "Get whatever you want, baby. This is Aunt Colita's store, so whatever you see that you want, you get it!" Seeking relief from the intense Houston heat, I would always make a beeline for the big, white ice cream freezer, gazing down through the sliding glass door into the irresistible variety of goodies until I decided what I wanted – usually an orange sherbet Push Up pop – and then sliding the door open to retrieve my selection. Then, I would head over to the chips, grab a nice big bag, and take them over to the checkout counter, where I would make my final selection: some Starburst or a pickle. While all of the other kids and their parents from the neighborhood were standing in line with their goodies, my aunt would see me waiting and just wave me ahead. "Come on up here, Shannon! Your Aunt Colita is going to get you a bag for all of your stuff. Is that all you want? Come on up here!"

My aunt would instruct whoever was working the counter to give me a bag, and then she would usher me to another part of the building where she operated a successful resale shop. Here, she would show me the finest name-brand bounty that she had collected over the past week or so, inviting me to take whatever I wanted. "Take whatever you want, but only if you're going to wear it! Can't nobody give your Aunt Colita nothing she don't want. If you don't like it, don't take it, but if you like it, you take whatever you want!" Aunt Colita continued with her generosity for several decades throughout my life, offering me armfuls of the best fashions, shoes and accessories, free of charge. As I would sift between the goods, she would carefully explain the quality that I was handling: Yves St. Laurent, Halston, Gucci, Calvin Klein, Valentino, Ralph Lauren, and more. As I excitedly worked my way through the racks, particularly after I became a fashion-forward adult, she would watch me with loving eyes while still cautioning me, "Take whatever you want, but only if you're going to wear it! Can't nobody give your Aunt Colita nothing she don't want. If you don't like it, don't take it, but if you like it, you take whatever you want!"

From the time I was a little girl who walked the blocks in Third Ward hand-in-hand with my Aunt Colita, watching others gaze upon her with respect and pride and admiring her position as an owner, I knew I wanted to be a boss. The highly-observant youngster that I was, I absorbed everything about her life, her lifestyle, her interactions with others, her privilege, and her power. Because of my experiences with her and my exposure to the possibilities that existed, I knew as a child that I wanted to own my own, work for myself, and have others work for me. From that time and for many years thereafter, entrepreneurship just made sense! It seemed to be a much better career option than working a traditional job and being subject to the orders and preferences of others. Without realizing it, my Aunt Colita not only ignited my passion to become an entrepreneur; the spark that was set aflame in me made me so zealous about business ownership that I became an entrepreneur evangelist!

❖

When life ignites a passion in you that is simply meant to be, it also has a way of fanning that flame into a full-blown inferno, stoking it through additional exposure and experiences that feed its ravenous appetite much the way oxygen fuels fire. After my initial exposure to entrepreneurship through my Aunt Colita, I encountered other impactful models that went on to shape and further define my entrepreneurial ambitions, some through observation from afar, and others from a more up close and personal vantage point.

For example, my maternal grandfather, George Simmons, was also an entrepreneur. Although I was familiar with "Paw-Paw," as we called him, we did not share a close relationship. He lived in Hammond, Louisiana, about a four-and-a-half hour drive from Houston, Texas, and trips to visit him were quite rare. The first time that I can remember realizing that he was actually an entrepreneur was when my family and I visited him when I was a junior in high school; I remember this vividly because my brother and I had to miss homecoming to make the trip. Because I had already developed such a fascination with entrepreneurship, my signals immediately started firing when I heard my mother explain the greatness of who he was – and why. You see, my grandfather was a prominent figure in the city of Hammond, Louisiana, so much so that he was given a key to the city. He owned a grocery and liquor store, a cab service, and several apartment complexes. Although I did not have a close relationship with my grandfather, I had a strong appreciation for the reason behind people's lofty levels of regard for him: he was a successful entrepreneur. As a result, he had earned the respect and favor of the townspeople. Most importantly, my levels of admiration for who he was and what he represented rose to new levels, helping to further fan the entrepreneurial flame that burned within me. Somewhere along the line, somehow, I knew that entrepreneurship was going to be in my future.

❖

Aside from my interactions and observations of entrepreneurial models early on in life, perhaps no other exposure solidified my entrepreneurial passions and desire to work in the field of entrepreneurship than the exposure that I received while a student at The University of Texas at Austin. It was here, amidst the rolling hills of the Forty Acres and the bustling crowds of students adorned in burnt orange, that I discovered the world of entrepreneurship at a whole new level, stirring my entrepreneurial passions to new heights that I never thought possible! When I entered The University as a freshman, the goal was not so much to establish a venture of my own; in fact, the goal was blatantly undefined. Like many other students who enter college, I did not really have a solid sense of what I wanted to do – and my numerous major changes were evidence of this. I just knew that my world would forever be that of developing small businesses – either my own or someone else's. However, I pushed these aspirations to the back recesses of my mind for the time being. As the expectation goes, now that I had entered college, it was time to choose a major and be trained on all that I needed to learn to land the perfect job. You know... a *real* job.

As an undergraduate at The University of Texas at Austin, I, like many other young Longhorns, was searching for what I wanted to be in life – with an ongoing urgency that fell just short of a panic. With every ticking second of every drawn-out semester, I realized that what I wanted to be in life was inextricably tied to my career selection and its corresponding course of study, so I could not approach it haphazardly. This decision was not simply about a list of courses. No, this was my entire *identity,* because, let's face it: in our nation, you are what you *do.* My entire identity was at stake, and it was hanging on the thread of my career selection.

In my career search, my academic major changes ran the gamut, and most of my student career years were spent in science-based fields: geophysical engineering, petroleum engineering, chemical engineering, for the first year and a half, and finally, chemistry for the next three years. I was fairly successful with each of these forays, though each one was as meaningless, boring, dull and uninspiring as the next. I chose these fields not out of my sincere interest in them but out of my perceived notion of their future revenue-generating potential. I knew I wouldn't necessarily be happy with my career, but at least I would not be living on my parents' sofa after I graduated. Cash is king, so I stuck with the sciences, despite my lack of fulfillment.

Though superfluously unmotivated, I spent my time majoring in chemistry and working in the chemistry department. Before long, I was awarded a prized and highly-coveted summer internship in chemistry that provided me with valuable hands-on experience and leadership training in the "real world." Little did I realize, until I was thrust into its belly, that the "real world" was overrated, and that the corporate life – especially one lived in a gray cubicle that was conspicuously hidden from even the faintest ray of sunshine – was just as dull, mind-numbing, and dreadful as the classes that prepared me for it. Each day felt like prison: I would wake up early, pack a lunch, crawl through traffic, sit in my cubicle amongst the miles of other endless cubicles, obey the orders and directions I was given, take the mandated lunch break at the mandated time, and then complete the rest of the day, only to crawl back home through the traffic to rest up so I could do it all over again the next day. The only thing that I did like was the money. However, as impressive as the check was, I knew that it was not worth it. Though I endured the summer internship, I completed it with an unquestioning awareness that the corporate cubicle life was not for me. But what *was*? And *where* in the heck *was* it?

Fresh off of my real job, real world experience, when fall registration rolled around, I deviated from my usual enrollment routine. I opted to register for classes that were out of my typical study plan, classes that were, in many respects, not highly-regarded by the engineering, science, government, pre-med and finance geeks on campus. Yes, I signed up for a class in sociology – one that actually interested me and made me want to go to class instead of skipping it to lounge in the lush grass on the tree-lined quad under the warm Texas sun. It was one of "*those* kinds of classes," the kind that you know you'll find interesting even though you can see no foreseeable way of leveraging such classes into any type of meaningful career.

It was in the Sociology Department in my first class of the year that I met professor emeritus John Sibley Butler in an introductory class entitled "Introduction to Entrepreneurship." After the first class, learning about the basic principles of entrepreneurship, middle-man theory, immigrant entrepreneurship, and the successes of entrepreneurs that had taken their destinies into their own hands, I was *hooked*! Every word spoken resounded with me and coaxed forward the entrepreneurial dream that I had pressed back into the dark recesses of my mind. As I slowly gathered my belongings and walked out of the auditorium classroom the very first day, I wore the biggest smile on my face because I knew that I had *finally* discovered my "it"! What was "it"? That thing for which I had been searching over the past four years to reignite passion. My "it" was entrepreneurship, just as it had been all along! As Ross said "It's *always* been you, Rach," to his beloved in the second season of the 90's television sitcom *Friends* ("The One with the

List" episode), I said to my beloved, "It's always been you, entrepreneurship!"

Each day that I sat in Dr. Butler's class, I grew more and more fascinated about the freedom and potentials that the entrepreneurial world offered to people of every race and ethnicity, gender, economic background, citizenship, and educational status. With each new day and each new lecture, my entrepreneurial flame grew more and more until it developed into an intense full-fledged scorching, blazing, brightly-colored inferno! Entrepreneurship *consumed* me until I graduated with my BA in 1996, and still continues to do so until this day. By the time I crossed the stage with my diploma, I was a fireball that incessantly encouraged all of my friends, family, and even strangers on the street to start their own businesses. I was an entrepreneur evangelist burning with passion!

Fast forward two years later to graduate school: I entered the doctoral program in Organizations & Occupations to study the science of new ventures directly under Dr. Butler. Dr. Butler was formerly the chair of the Sociology department, but was now chairman of the Management department in the renowned University of Texas McCombs School of Business. I was living the dream with each advanced entrepreneurial class that this seasoned entrepreneurial expert taught, eagerly anticipating every word of wisdom and every lesson he would share that was birthed out of his academic training, research and entrepreneurial experience. However, no presentation, no lecture and no guest speaker impacted me like Dr. Butler's introduction to business incubation. I still have my treasured yellow spiral single-subject notebook (with its corresponding syllabus still tucked inside), now frayed at its edges as a result of frequent reference, into which I painstakingly noted the contents of each lecture. Almost prophetically, I predicted that I would be referring to its rich content for years to come, and years later, I still am.

The day that I was first introduced to the concept of business incubation, the introduction was coupled with an extensive discussion about risk. This was a natural partnering of topics because the entrepreneur is often portrayed as a risk taker and incubators help to mitigate risk. This particular day, however, I learned that entrepreneurs were not risk takers! Why? Because they are so sure that whatever they are doing will succeed that they tend not to perceive what they are doing as "risky"! What's more, if they do perceive that there is a risk in the venture that they are undertaking, they simply continue to add on creativity, engage in further innovation, and conduct more trial research until the "risk" is no longer a threat. However, although entrepreneurs tend to actually engage in risk-reduction, society in general perceives the development of new ventures to be quite a risky proposition. That said, the discussion turned to the topic of entities called "business incubators": organizations that allowed entrepreneurs to manage their perceived risk by providing them with various safeguards and support networks designed to hedge their risk and nearly *guarantee* their success. Simply put, incubators manage risk so effectively that, in a sense, the risk is virtually eliminated for the entrepreneur!

Imagine how this would have sounded to me, the entrepreneurial evangelist. Because I was an academic researcher, I already knew that four out of five small businesses would close their doors before they were five years old. To learn that entities could be developed to obliterate this failure rate and guarantee entrepreneurial success was music to my ears – and during these lectures, I was *all* ears! I sat on the edge of my seat and absorbed every word.

I listened with intrigue, fascination and amazement as Dr. Butler gave the full run-down on business incubators. These (at the time) little-known entities provided office space, human resources, technology, access to information, access to capital, access to know-how networks, and access to anything else that an entrepreneur needed to go from fledgling start-up to full power jet-engine speed in record time. Next came the jaw-dropping statistics about the successes of business incubators, particularly that 87-93% of incubated small businesses are still open after five years as compared with only 20% of non-incubated businesses.[1] Even after five years, significantly more non-incubated businesses failed than those that were incubated. Incubators virtually guaranteed an entrepreneur's success!

Surrounded by my business school classmates who diligently took notes on their laptops and notepads with occasional indifferent gazes towards the professor, I also tried to keep a straight face and maintain my composure... but I was *bursting* inside! If truth be told, my face grew hot, and I felt flushed; the fire was burning so brightly inside of me that I thought I might *combust* at any moment! Sitting here learning about business incubation was undeniably one of the most exciting moments of my life! From my perspective, for an entrepreneur to have access to a business incubator was akin to having access to the fairy godmother of the business world. I imagined this fairy godmother helping to fulfill or compensate for every possible need or shortcoming that stood in the path between the entrepreneur and the ultimate fulfillment of his or her business dream. Despite my over-the-top enthusiasm, I was able to hold it together enough to take copious notes and eventually file out of the class with my entrepreneurial fervor undetected.

Upon learning about business incubation, I was filled with awe at the prospect of pioneering the push to establish these business birthing centers all around the world. After all, if an incubator virtually guaranteed the success of an early-stage business by providing for it all of the nurture, protection and resources it needed to survive and thrive on its own – much like a mother hen would do with her baby chicks – why wouldn't we work to put *at least* one in *every* community? I felt like running to the top of a mountain and shouting, "Let's build business incubators, people, and here's how we're gonna do it!" Yes, it was just that thrilling to me. No exaggeration.

I was so captivated by the idea of business incubation that it finally gave my burning passion a brand name and my entrepreneurial research a focus. My newly-focused passion was to answer two questions: 1) What does it take to develop the most effective business incubator possible? and 2) How can communities and nonprofit organizations utilize business incubation to nurture and develop new ventures that will in turn help to economically develop the community or nonprofit organization that supported their success?

With these questions constantly occupying the forefront of my consciousness, when I was faced with the question of what my doctoral dissertation topic would be, the choice was obvious and clear – a no-brainer. It would be about business incubation. The formal title of my doctoral dissertation eventually became *Business Incubation as an Economic Development Tool in Emerging Markets*. To collect data, simply making a phone call or two to the incubators listed in the

International Business Innovation Association's (InBIA, known as the National Business Incubation Association at the time) directory would not do. Instead, I hopped on a plane and traveled around the United States to visit various not-for-profit (slightly different than for-profit) business incubators from Los Angeles to Portland, from Philadelphia to Cleveland, from Houston to Atlanta, and from Birmingham to Raleigh-Durham. In my travels, I took behind-the-scenes tours of the incubators, interviewed the key managers/directors and entrepreneur tenants, sat in on meetings, collected materials, examined their processes, and gathered first-hand data on what did and did not work to effectively incubate entrepreneurs. I was especially curious to discover what was *supposed* to work, according to textbook theory, for incubators in general that did not *actually* work in practice for nonprofit business incubators, considering the budgetary restrictions under which nonprofits often operate.

The research goal was this: to deconstruct the systems, procedures, operations and make-ups of several successful incubators in urban areas in order to construct a business model of an incubator that could be used in economic development zones nationwide – a best practices type of study, if you will. The research design utilized to structure the data collection, analysis and summary is an adaptation of a reverse design process popular in academic research.

The results of this national research study, combined with hundreds of hours of data mining from other research-based sources, are the content that I am pleased to present in this book. In this presentation of the results, however, I focus not on the economic development aspect of business incubation, but rather on the basics: what are business incubators, what are they good for, and how can an organization build an effective one to nurture and hedge the successes of small businesses in their community. Perhaps it is because of my passionate love for the idea of business incubation (especially since I have seen so many successful incubators in action) that I believe that anyone and everyone should be on the incubator bandwagon. Then again, this would not be the first time I've been called idealistic about something. I'm not put off by this.

I happen to be of the persuasion described by novelist Alisa Steinberg who once wrote: "Being an idealist is not being a simpleton;

without idealists there would be no optimism and without optimism there would be no courage to achieve advances that so-called realists would have you believe could never come to fruition." I truly believe that our society can, with the help of communities, local governments, churches, and other nonprofit entities, establish incubators that can produce successful entrepreneurs with a social conscience that drives them to reinvest their profits into the nonprofit entities that invested in their success, spurring economic growth at rates like never before.

❖

To understand business incubation is to love business incubation. That is to say, to learn about the successes that business incubation can ensure for new ventures is to want to incubate an entrepreneur – or to want to be incubated if you, yourself are an entrepreneur. In fact, whenever I have the opportunity to explain to others what business incubators are and how they work, whether they are entrepreneurs or not, they become just as enthusiastic as I am. Their responses are always the same: "Wow! That's seems like it would be an entrepreneur's dream come true. Why wouldn't *every* entrepreneur want to take their new venture into an incubator?" If it's a small business owner that I am talking to, their responses tend to be a bit different: "*Really*? These places exist? Why haven't I heard of them? How can I *find* one of these incubators for my business... *fast*?!" I know the feeling. I feel the same way, and soon, after reading this book, I hope you will too.

Several years ago, when the primary data collection for this research study was completed, when one typed in "business incubation" as a search term, the search yielded very few mainstream resources. In fact, there were almost none. Amazingly, years later, the same is still true: simply typing in "business incubation" on Amazon, the nation's largest bookseller, will yield scarce results for those interested in learning about business incubation and even fewer results for how to establish a formal business incubator in one's own community. Formal business incubation will become one of the most important means of economic and community development in our society, particularly when the process is engaged in the context of cultivating disenfranchised urban communities, or emerging markets. As such, it is critical that research-based resources be developed to empower entities interested in nurturing new ventures with knowledge on how to create business incubators that are driven by a mission to build businesses that will in turn help to build their communities.

It is not enough to merely call for microenterprise development in emerging markets; we must become champions for these key contributors to our local economies, ensuring that we are fully vested in the processes that are proven to result in their success. When local microenterprises are successful, we are all successful. Strong entrepreneurs build strong businesses. Strong businesses build strong economies. Strong economies build strong communities. Thus, the key to laying the proper groundwork for strong communities is an investment in the entrepreneur. The best investment: incubation.

❖

I could not complete this Introduction without paying homage to the mother of all incubator organizations, which has been the leader in incubator research for the past 30 years: the International Business Innovation Association, or the InBIA. I should note that at the time my research was conducted, the organization was known as the National Business Incubation Association (NBIA), and it was located in Athens, Ohio. However, in 2015, the organization rebranded itself as the InBIA in an effort to better reflect its membership and mission to advance global entrepreneurship and incubation.[2] Thus, if you are a business incubation or entrepreneurship researcher and come across the name NBIA or any articles or materials produced by or about the NBIA, know that these resources were produced prior to September 2015. As you see references throughout this book to the NBIA, know that they are attributed to the NBIA for this reason. Also, if you attempt to link to any of these resources in the NBIA archives or to visit the NBIA website, you will most likely receive an error message, because the nbia.org website no longer exists. However, no worries! Simply visit inbia.org to request access to the resources you need, and one of their staff members will be glad to assist.

The InBIA seeks to advance the business creation process to increase entrepreneurial success and individual opportunity, strengthening communities worldwide. Its mission is to help guide, mentor and develop sustainable entrepreneur support programs in every industry and demographic around the globe. The InBIA operates with a goal of enriching the entire ecosystem by providing industry resources, education, events and global programming to help their members better serve the needs of their unique communities and regions. Now headquartered in Orlando, Florida, the InBIA is the world's leading organization advancing business incubation and entrepreneurship. Through various conferences, education and training, advocacy, research and publications, industry news and resources, and designations and accreditations, the InBIA provides excellent resources for business incubator managers, developers, and supporters and is comprised of more than 1900 members, including incubator partners, influencers and ecosystem builders, in more than 60 nations.[3] If you are going to establish a business incubator, you would be well-advised to join the InBIA.

I would also be remiss if I neglected to point readers towards another excellent resource available for those desiring to nurture and develop small businesses: the Ewing Marion Kauffman Foundation for Entrepreneurship. More targeted towards the entrepreneur than the incubator developer, Kauffman drives research, policy, innovation and the education of entrepreneurs. Established in the mid-1960s by the late entrepreneur and philanthropist Ewing Marion Kauffman, the foundation's vision is to foster "a society of economically independent individuals who are engaged citizens, contributing to the improvement of their communities." The Kauffman Foundation executes this primarily through making grants and targeting its operations towards advancing entrepreneurship and improving the education of children and youth. Practically everyone who works in the field of entrepreneurship is familiar with the Kauffman Foundation, as it is the world's largest foundation devoted to entrepreneurship. Since you are journeying into the field of entrepreneurship, the Kauffman Foundation is an organization you should know.

I remember when I was given the opportunity to participate in a research project with the Kauffman Foundation as a graduate student. Of course, from the time I was an undergraduate studying entrepreneurship all the way through my doctoral studies, I had read and researched all things Kauffman, including the life of the founder, the great Ewing Marion Kauffman. Mr. Kauffman, one of the most innovative and successful entrepreneurs of his time, developed the Kauffman Foundation to change the lives of young people through education, particularly those from disadvantaged backgrounds. He believed the key to achieving this was enterprise development, as it would help young people to realize their individual potential while simultaneously stimulating the economy. Even today, two words define the mission of the Kauffman Foundation: education and entrepreneurship.

At the time, my doctoral supervisor's Blackberry overflowed with other commitments that prohibited him from attending a planning meeting at Kauffman in Kansas City, Missouri. My supervisor was tasked with representing The University of Texas for a big national entrepreneurship research project that was to soon be launched. Ever the favored graduate student with a fiery passion for all things entrepreneurial, he chose me to represent him in his stead. Upon hearing that I was going to Kauffman, I was *ecstatic*; this was Kauffman, after all! For an entrepreneurship researcher, this was, in a manner of speaking, like going to the entrepreneurship mecca. I was so proud to be given the honor of sitting around the table with some of the greatest entrepreneurship research and development minds in the nation. This was one of the most defining moments of my tenure as a graduate student, providing me a glimpse into what my future as a champion of entrepreneurship would be.

❖

In closing, this book is written for the business student, community organization, local government, nonprofit entity, community and economic developer, church or religious organization or other social do-gooder desiring to learn, in practical language, how to establish a local nonprofit business incubator (although the principles can also be utilized in constructing for-profit incubators as well). It is my goal to transfer my entrepreneurial passion to you through the pages of this book so that you can, in turn, use your own passion as a driving force to nurture and develop strong, sustainable microenterprises all around the world. It is my hope that by the end of this book, you have a solid understanding of what it takes to nurture, build and grow thriving entrepreneurs and their microenterprises through business incubation, not only for the sake of helping them realize their entrepreneurial dreams, but for the sake of the contributions they can make towards developing your community. One day, I look forward to reading about how you have utilized the incubator development blueprint in this book to become some struggling entrepreneur's fairy godmother of the business world, granting them everything they need to realize their business success!

1

Making a Case for Business Incubation

The Rationale & the History of Incubators

Before any discussion about formal business incubation can be discussed in context, it is first necessary to understand the origin and background of formal business incubation. Indeed, most people that I encounter have never heard of business incubation; although these business birthing centers have been present among us for years, they have flown under the radar for the most part, leaving the general public largely unfamiliar with the concept. However, where did incubators originate, how were they run, and when did nurturing new ventures through these entities begin? Who saw the initial need for the development of a formal business incubator, and are incubators still organized around those same needs today? What rationale even exists behind the concept of co-locating entrepreneurs in a formal office setting to share support networks, information, and resources for their mutual growth and development? To answer these questions, we will first undertake a theoretical examination of the logic of the incubator as a formal organization and then examine a broad overview of the history of business incubation in the United States.

Why Develop a Formal Incubator?
Establishing the Rationale with Organizational Theory

If you desire to nurture the new ventures of start-up entrepreneurs, this process can be more effectively and efficiently carried out through a formal business incubator organization than through individual efforts. Simply put, incubator organizations can get more done for entrepreneurs with fewer resources than individuals can. However, for academicians or researchers who are unable to endorse the legitimacy of a process or idea without first viewing it through the lens of a theoretical construct, I begin with introducing the use of business incubator organizations as a logical choice to cultivate entrepreneurs through the framework of Organizational Theory.

Decades of Organizational Theory research have helped us to understand the following:

1. **Organizations can offer greater efficiency and productivity when executing operations.**

The costs and benefits of creating organizations are evident when organizations are compared with alternative social forms for carrying on complex work.[4]   The utility of an organization in many cases outweighs the efficiency and productivity of individual task accomplishment when complex operations need to be executed.

In layman's language: If a process requiring more than one task needs to be done, we are more likely to produce the results we desire if we engage our efforts collectively as a group than if we work alone, and we will end up spending less time and fewer resources along the way.

The bottom line: Together, we can get more done... faster and with fewer resources!

2. Organizations can often accomplish what individuals cannot accomplish working alone.

In many circumstances, there are some things that individuals cannot do outside of the context of a formal organization. According to Parsons, "The development of organizations is the principal mechanism by which, in a highly differentiated society, it is possible to 'get things done,' to achieve goals beyond the reach of the individual." [5]

In layman's language: There are some things you can accomplish working by yourself, but there are other things you will only be able to accomplish if you work with others, no matter how hard you try to do them alone. Every now and then, you'll have goals that will necessitate the help, support, and contributions of others!

The bottom line: Sometimes the Lone Ranger rode alone, but other times he had to bring along Tonto to get the job done.

3. Organizations can help us accomplish complex tasks and achieve shared goals.

Whereas organizations emerged having a communal form based on the bonds of kinship and personal ties, with time, the organization as we know it came to be characterized more by associative forms based on contractual arrangements among individuals having no ties other than a willingness to pursue shared interests or ends. [6] These arrangements have proven to be effective in accomplishing the completion of complex tasks, one of the prime benefits of working within an organization versus as an individual to achieve a common goal.

In layman's language: One benefit of us working together to accomplish the same challenging goal is that you and I actually formally agree that we're going to work on it together so that we can successfully meet our goal. This benefits us both.

The bottom line: If you and I are on a long, unfamiliar journey trying to get to the same destination, especially on an unpaved road, we should ride together instead of taking separate cars, don't you think?

4. Organizations' centralized communications improve performance and efficiency.

One of the most prominent explanations for rationalizing the benefit of organizations over individualization is that of the efficient information processing that organizations offer. This explanation for the emergence of organizations centers on their superior efficiency in managing flows of information, resulting in a centralized communication system. Early research on communication structures examined the effects of centralized vs. decentralized communications networks on the task performance of groups. These, and other research studies, consistently report results revealing that individuals working in a more centralized structure are more efficient in their performance. [7]

In layman's language: When you work with others instead of by yourself, not only can you receive greater quantities of information faster, you can receive it from a wider variety of sources in a more organized fashion than pulling it from here and there as it comes in – and this helps you work smarter, more efficiently, and more productively.

The bottom line: It costs you less in time and energy resources to go to one secretary to get all of your messages than to walk around to all of your associates' offices and get them yourself one by one.

5. Organizations offer greater time and cost efficiency than many individual operations.

Working as an individual could likely cost a person more than it would cost if he sought to accomplish the same task utilizing the collective efforts and resources of an organization. Consider this, for example, in light of the efficiency of group vs. individual communication structures. Arrow writes: "Since transmission of information is costly, in the sense of using resources, especially the time of individuals, it is cheaper and more efficient to transmit all the pieces of information once to a central place than to disseminate each of them to everyone."[8]

In layman's language: In terms of resources, it often costs more for an individual to work alone than it does to work with others, and this applies to the cost of both time and money.

The bottom line: Things cost less when you buy them in bulk than when you buy them individually.

Considering these tenets of Organizational Theory, one can reasonably justify an argument that forming an organization is the best way to efficiently accomplish a defined set of common goals or interests; the pursuit of goals and interests as an individual would demonstrate a lack of resourcefulness and jeopardize the likelihood of the individual attaining a certain goal or achieving a particular outcome. Especially when these goals and interests are heavily reliant upon the gathering and dissemination of information and resources, a more centralized, stable structure, such as that of an organization, is the more certain, reliable and effective means to realize a desired outcome, or accomplish a certain goal or objective.

The same argument holds true for the formal business incubator organization. There are clear benefits to the co-location of start-ups in a centralized resource-based support organization during the infancy and early-stage phases of their growth and development. This is particularly true when compared to the alternative: a rugged individualist approach that offers them only limited access, if any, to the support networks and resources essential for both their short- and long-term viability. Formal business incubator organizations, primarily due to the centralization of the information and resources they can offer to start-ups, help to ensure the growth and viability of the entrepreneur. The rates of growth and development of entrepreneurs nurtured in incubator organizations are proven to be significantly higher than the rates experienced by entrepreneurs operating individually.

A History of Business Incubators
in the United States

While it would be wonderful to report that from the start, business incubators were developed as a means to ensure the success of new start-ups through the provision of resources, networking, and capital, such an account would be untrue; business incubators had no such noble mission of providing business assistance when they were initially created. History records that the first incubator in the world was developed for quite a different reason. In 1959, Charles Mancuso & Son, Inc. purchased a huge multi-story 850,000 square foot building, previously owned by Johnston Harvester and later Massey-Ferguson (which manufactured harvester combines), in Batavia, New York that also came with 30 acres of land. Although the prominent family owned a number of various local businesses, some family members wondered if this latest acquisition was a wise investment. They paid $180,000 for the building, which had been vacant for a few years, and it was evident that it would require a considerable amount of renovation, especially with the massive roof that needed to be completely replaced. The family knew that they would need to invest much more to restore the facility before it could be utilized, and they selected Joseph Mancuso to assess their options concerning what to do with the new facility and to figure out how they might make a profit from their purchase.[9]

Mancuso originated what is considered today to be a revolutionary idea: he rented the building out to business tenants, allowing them to occupy as much space as they needed for their operations. It was Mancuso's goal to fill the big, empty building, hoping to find enough tenants to guarantee that the facility would reach an occupancy rate that would produce a profit for the family's investment. The first known tenant in the Batavia, New York building was a sign painter that took up only 2,000 square feet of the 850,000 available square feet. The first year of the building's operation, Mancuso only managed to secure 20 to 30 tenants who utilized approximately 90,000 square feet. The building was reportedly always on the verge of financial trouble, though it leased some of its available space as a warehouse and other spaces for service providers and a number of other types of businesses.[10] Thus, the first known business incubator was born of economic necessity. Although it allowed tenants of the building to share the expense of various office services, the intent of the incubator was not that of providing business assistance.

The idea soon caught on as more and more people became aware of Mancuso's development strategy and its potential impact on economic development and job creation in their own communities. Implementing such a program established Mancuso as the father of business incubators, and he is also credited with inventing the term "incubator." Mancuso commented, "I brought in a company from Connecticut that incubated chickens. I used to kid about it. I'd tell people we were incubating chickens. Pretty soon it was known as a business incubator. I didn't set out to invent it!""[11]

Over the years, the incubator, now known as the Batavia Industrial Center, has housed thousands of businesses in millions of square feet of old buildings in Batavia, leading to the creation of countless jobs. Today, the incubator boasts about 110 tenants. About 1,000 people work in the building which is now run by Mancuso's three sons.

> *I brought in a company from Connecticut that incubated chickens. I used to kid about it. I'd tell people we were incubating chickens. Pretty soon, it was known as a business incubator. I didn't set out to invent it!*
>
> **- JOSEPH MANCUSO,**
> **THE FATHER OF BUSINESS INCUBATION**

The incubator does not function like traditional business incubators as we know them today. Although the center continues to encourage entrepreneurship and start-ups, anyone can lease space in the Batavia

Industrial Center. Even further, they can stay as long as they want, for there is no graduation or exit policy as one would find in a traditional business incubator. For this reason, some businesses have been in the Batavia Industrial Center's incubator for more than 30 years.

While Mancuso is considered the "father of the business incubator," the first formal business incubator to host a business incubation program developed for the express purpose of assisting start-up and early-stage businesses was established around 1980 at Rensselaer Polytechnic Institute, an initiative of George Low who was to become the future president of Rensselaer. The Rensselaer Polytechnic program was revolutionary in that it endeavored to expose students to entrepreneurship in a laboratory setting, by bringing in guest speakers to talk about how to start a business, pairing students with local businesses in apprenticeship positions, and linking student and faculty entrepreneurs to potential investors. Armed with such strong support resources, companies began to be launched by both students and faculty alike. Originally housed in space available on the Rensselaer campus, the school's incubator now occupies two facilities, each consisting of 40,000 square feet of space. Today, the Rensselaer incubator continues to successfully produce graduate companies for students, faculty, and community residents who desire to start their own business enterprises. [12]

With the industry experiencing unprecedented growth, today, there are more than 1,400 business incubators in North America, up from only 12 such organizations existing in 1980. [13] Incubators originally appeared during the recession that occurred during the early 1980's when large corporations shut down, leaving behind empty plants and thousands of jobless residents. Having observed the opportunities that small business incubators presented for alleviating economic distress in other areas, civic, community and economic development groups began to renovate these empty spaces that lay idle in their own neighborhoods, transforming them into enterprise centers that could house and mentor entrepreneurs, create new job opportunities, and generate income for investors, service providers and the community. [14]

The average incubator was established in 1991, and one new incubator opens up in the United States every week. [15] Over time, however, not only has the number of incubators grown, but the number of client companies and graduates has climbed as well. More than 8,000 small start-up firms currently reside in incubators, and more than 4,500 existing businesses have graduated from incubator programs. Today, incubator organizations are offering more services to clients than ever before, serving an average of 35 clients (resident and affiliate combined; average number of resident clients served is 20). Incubators are also offering more specialized services to their residents and affiliates, depending on their clients' unique needs. In 2011, incubators in North America assisted nearly 49,000 start-up companies, which provided full-time employment for almost 200,000 workers. Further, these incubated businesses helped the incubators in which they were housed accomplish their economic development goals by generating an annual revenue of nearly $15 billion, helping to drive the U.S. economy and contribute to the economies of their local communities.[16]

2

Definitions, Distinctions & Demands

What a Business Incubator *Is* and What It *Is Not*

Thousands of entrepreneurs have strategically located their start-up and early-stage ventures in business incubators for one primary reason: to increase the chances of their business' growth and viability. Despite this fact, however, the concept of formal business incubation is relatively unknown to the average citizen. What is more surprising, however, is how few people who operate in the business world, including entrepreneurs, have no knowledge of business incubators. For formal business incubators to be such proven, effective vehicles in driving start-up viability and entrepreneurial business success, the numbers of those in the business arena who can explain what an incubator is and does is astonishingly low. This results in business incubators remaining somewhat of an obscure, hidden, and consequently, underutilized resource in North America.

Many people are so unaware of the existence of incubators as business-building organizations that upon first hearing the term "incubator," their initial thought is "Isn't that a place for baby chickens?" Granted, it can be challenging to unite the terms "business" and "incubator" into one phrase without offering further explanation. In fact, almost without fail, each time someone asks about my area of research, the dialogue goes something like this:

Them: *"So, what is your area of research?"*
Me: *"Business incubation."*
Them: *(after several moments of silent contemplation and a look of bewilderment) "Oh, okay... so now... what exactly is that?"*

Defining Formal Business Incubation

A standard, textbook definition of a business incubator is:

Business incubators *help entrepreneurs translate their ideas into sustainable businesses by guiding them through the maze of starting and growing a thriving business.* [17]

A more user-friendly, layman's definition that I often use to define formal business incubators is:

*A **formal business incubator** is an organization known to provide office or production space, business and technical assistance, access to capital, support services, and other resources in a nurturing environment that significantly increases the likelihood of growth and viability for a start-up, early-stage, or existing business.*

Simply put, a business incubator is an organization that provides the resources and support needed to cultivate new businesses to the point that they are viable (they can live and thrive on their own). Incubators decrease the probability of business failure and increase the likelihood that a business will succeed by feeding it exactly what it needs in its early stages of development. The investment that incubators make into their businesses activates certain growth mechanisms in the enterprise so that entrepreneurs not only realize success, but they realize greater levels of success in much less time than it would take for them to attain it on their own. In fact, industry professionals also refer to incubators by other labels such as "catalysts" or "accelerators," for these organizations are a means to speed up the growth and development of start-up and early-stage businesses (although we will soon learn that these terms should *not* be used synonymously with the term "incubator").

Various researchers help to enlighten our understanding of what defines formal business incubation, including its intended purpose and function. According to the International Business Innovation Association, business incubation provides entrepreneurs with the expertise, networks and tools that they need to make their ventures successful. Incubation programs also diversify economies, commercialize technologies, create jobs and build wealth.[18] According to Greene and Butler, the purpose of an incubator is to provide some combination of resources necessary to nurture a new or early-stage business to a level of maturity at which it can survive on its own.[19] Gibbons provided another characterization of what an business incubator is, explaining, "Incubators are something like a mixture of an office park and a business school for entrepreneurs."[20] Overall, researchers generally agree that business incubators help to equip entrepreneurs with the training, resources and support they need in order to grow and survive on their own so they can create jobs and contribute to local economies.

Considering all notions, the ultimate definition, purpose, and function of business incubators can be summed up in this: incubator organizations assist start-up and early-stage businesses by providing resources that these small enterprises might not otherwise be able to access due to their lack of knowledge, capital, or networks. Because of the resources they offer to early-stage entrepreneurs, these organizations serve as a major source of growth and economic development for communities.

> *The problem with most incubators*
> *is that most "incubators" are not incubators at all!*

What an Incubator Is *Not*

As you enter into the world of formal business incubation, it is vitally important to have a clear understanding of what an incubator is and what it is not. Without an accurate understanding of what it means to develop an actual business incubator, well-meaning individuals and business development entities will develop organizations and programs that house entrepreneurs, work with entrepreneurs, teach entrepreneurs, fund entrepreneurs, and even coach entrepreneurs, without actually developing an actual incubator organization. Many groups and entities claim to have opened a business incubator, when in actuality, they have merely opened another small business resource center or office park. What a formal incubator offers to its residents is far more comprehensive; each of the varied products it offers works in concert to ensure the success of the entrepreneur.

Business incubators expansively address many of the unique challenges that entrepreneurs face in the early stages of developing their microenterprises, including problems of high information costs, low service levels, difficulties in obtaining business services, and shortages of capital sources.[21] Incubator developers who desire to nurture the new ventures of entrepreneurs should note that there are marked differences between formal business incubation programs that can address these unique needs and other programs, entities, and organizations that also work with entrepreneurs. These "others" include small business development centers (SBDCs), investment groups, and even real estate holders that co-locate various small businesses in the same building. The chief differentiating element between formal business incubators and these entities is the level of support, buy-in, and responsibility that a business incubator program provides for the businesses housed in its facilities compared to the level that other organizations and entities provide. In order to further establish a clear understanding of the differences between actual business incubators and other entrepreneur support programs and organizations, it helps to understand the limitations of what these "other" organizations and entities offer to entrepreneurs.

First are Small Business Development Centers (SBDCs), which, although rich with resources for entrepreneurs, are not business incubators. These business assistance centers, which were established by the Small Business Administration and signed into law in 1980, provide management and technical assistance to aspiring entrepreneurs and small business owners. The SBDC network is comprised of partnerships between the U.S. Congress, the Small Business Administration, various organizations within the private sector, educational institutions, and state governments. Consulting services offered by SBDCs are free, and trainings are offered at-cost. Entrepreneurs can visit one of nearly 1,000 SBDCs throughout the nation as often as their needs require to receive face-to-face business consulting in areas including business plan development, licensing and regulatory compliance, advertising, marketing, branding, where and how to access capital, and international trade regulations, among others. SBDCs are an extremely vital resource to entrepreneurs and provide consulting, training, management and technical assistance to nearly one million aspiring and existing small business owners every year.[22] However, despite all that they offer, SBDCs are not business incubators; they simply help entrepreneurs to help themselves by pointing the way as opposed to leading the way. It's like the difference between showing someone a map and explaining how to get from point A to point B and actually grabbing the person by the hand and saying "Look, this is where *we* are, and here's the plan to get to where *we're* going. Now, come on! I'm *taking* you to point B. If you don't let go of my hand, *we* are going to get there together!"

Second are investment groups, which, although they play a major role in helping businesses to grow with the financial resources and mentoring that they offer, are not business incubators. Investment groups have a self-interested motive: finding promising early-stage businesses, providing them with the funding they need to grow their businesses, and hedging their investment in the business by building in protective mechanisms to ensure the business' success. Investment groups rarely, if ever, fund start-ups in their infancy. That is to say, if aspiring entrepreneurs merely have what they deem to be a good business idea and go to an investment group seeking funding, the chances that the group will fund the entrepreneur are slim to none. Instead, in order to be awarded funding from investment groups, a business must already be functional, have some sales, be able to show that its idea has been tested and is in demand by the market, etc. In other words, it has to be an already-functional early-stage business that shows promise. That said, when investment groups step into the picture, they assume that the entrepreneurs already have the basic knowledge and framework for how to operate the business, because the business is already operational and has already achieved some measure of success.

More often than not, major capital infusions come with strings; as a condition of taking their money, the investment group will require that an executive of their choosing take the helm of the business' operations or at least play a key role in decision making for the early-stage business. These executives are typically knowledgeable, trained, and experienced players in the business world that possess the know-how for accelerating the growth and visibility of the business in the market, maximizing the use of the investment that the group has made into the business. However, while capital infusions and expert business leadership contribute to the growth and development of start-up and early-stage businesses, the investment groups that selectively provide them are not business incubators. Many other resources are needed to effectively incubate a business. Campbell supports this thought, noting that "though some investment groups call themselves incubators, they offer no guidance, expertise, services or other forms of nurturing".[23]

In this case, it's like the difference between an investment company saying "Let us assist you by giving you the capital you need, letting our guys take the reins of your business, and growing your business for you while you watch," and an incubator saying "We'll help you get the money for your company, and then we'll provide you with the training, guidance, technical assistance and mentoring that you need to leverage every dollar for the growth and development of your business' success." In the case of the investment group's assistance, it's about them, their money, and hedging their investment in the business. In the case of the incubator's assistance, it's about the entrepreneur, building the entrepreneur's knowledge and expertise, and ensuring the entrepreneur's success. Some might take the position, "Success is all about the money! Who cares whether the investment group takes over, starts making the decisions, and runs the company as long as it's making money?"

I know many entrepreneurs who would take those to task who believe that relinquishing control of their business, standing on the sidelines watching as someone else runs their operations, and merely cashing a check makes them successful. Lots of entrepreneurs want to maintain control of their own companies while being empowered with the financial resources, training, and mentoring they need to attain their goals and realize success. Business incubators often allow them the opportunity to do so by providing them with access to capital resources that do not require exchanging their dream of running their own successful business as a condition.

The final type of entity that is most commonly misperceived as a business incubator is that of a building or facility housing a number of small businesses. People who are introduced to the concept of business incubation on a surface level will often make this mistake; they see a significant clustering of small businesses housed in one facility and call it a business incubator. This, in fact, is not the case. The mere co-location of a group of businesses in one building or facility does not make the entity an incubator any more than the co-location of a group of police officers in one place makes the place a police station; it could be a doughnut shop!

> The mere co-location of a group of businesses
> in one building or facility does not make the entity
> an incubator any more than the co-location of a group
> of police officers in one place makes the place a
> police station; it could be a doughnut shop!

Platform 9

I cannot emphasize enough that office buildings, executive suites, or other facilities that merely house multiple small businesses together are *not* business incubators! A more accurate label for them would be "real estate operations targeted toward small businesses." These organizations most often act only as landlords to entrepreneurs, renting out scalable space for them to conduct their operations, from a couple of hundred square feet to a collection of office suites, or perhaps even a whole warehouse. Some of these real estate operations might even try to add value to what they offer their residents by providing access to shared resources within the facility and/or offering workshops and trainings designed to increase residents' business development aptitudes, they are still not, by definition, business incubators. Again, while the features these entities offer are typically found in business incubators, the presence of these features does not automatically qualify them as business incubators. Business incubators have a more comprehensive level of offerings that are strategically and systematically designed to complement one another for the growth and development of the start-up or early-stage venture.

What Is a Business Incubator?

Those seeking to develop genuine, legitimate business incubation programs must be careful to understand the differentiation between small business assistance centers, investment groups, real estate operations, and other entities and organizations that have the appearance of being business incubators without actually being business incubators. Otherwise, they will find themselves sinking their often-limited resources into the development of an organization that is poorly structured and ill-equipped to accomplish their purpose of effectively incubating new ventures.

The Six Defining Components
of a Formal Business Incubation Program

There are six defining components that should be present to qualify a program as a formal business incubator:

1. Facilities with Shared Resources
2. Training Program
3. Technical Assistance
4. Access to Networks
5. Coaching / Mentoring
6. A Champion

According to the NBIA's 2012 State of the Business Incubation Industry report, the components that ranked as most important to incubator clients were help with business basics, high-speed internet access, marketing assistance, and networking activities, although providing assistance with accessing funding and providing connections to specialized resources and connections were also reported as being important to incubator clients.[24] Thus, in order to meet clients' needs and incubate them effectively, an incubator must provide a comprehensive program that integrates each of these components.

what businesses seek

Facilities with Shared Resources

Formal business incubators typically offer their residents below-market rate office space to house their businesses. The spaces are often scalable, allowing businesses to start with a smaller space and expand the amount of space they occupy or migrate to larger spaces within the incubator as their growth demands or reduce the amount of space they occupy as their need for space decreases.

Leases are typically flexible in business incubators. Incubator managers realize that the future of a small business can be a challenge to predict; the business might grow at a rate faster than anticipated and need to exit the incubator for a larger space to house its operations, and this might require the entrepreneur to break his or her lease before its official end date. On the other hand, a company might go out of business before the end of its lease, also requiring the entrepreneur to break his or her lease with the business incubator.

The types of spaces that business residents occupy within an incubator can vary and are contingent upon the physical construction and build-out of the incubator itself. Some incubators are more finished and offer commercial-looking professional office spaces, while other incubators might be more industrial and offer unfinished spaces that can be used for manufacturing, wood or metalworking, or other production needs. Still, other incubator facilities might offer a combination of the two types of spaces, allowing companies to simultaneously occupy professional office space for operations and unfinished space for their production and/or storage needs.

Formal business incubators typically offer the following shared resources to entrepreneurs in their facilities (features may vary from incubator to incubator):

- Office space
- Office furniture
- Reception areas
- Conference rooms
- Meeting rooms
- Break rooms / Dining facilities
- Storage space

The shared resources that business incubators offer to their residents are an attractive offering to many entrepreneurs. These resources are often perks that start-up and early-stage entrepreneurs are seldom able to afford on their own. However, when entrepreneurs are placed in an incubator context in which their resources can be pooled together, because each business contributes a little towards each of these shared resources, all of the entrepreneurs can afford to access them. For example, one of the most appealing shared resources offered in many incubators is that of a receptionist. When they were working out of their home, garage, or local coffee shop, entrepreneurs performed their own receptionist work; they made their own phone calls, answered their own incoming calls, made their own copies, arranged their own deliveries, greeted their own visiting guests, and did the bulk of their own reception work. They did it all themselves, not because they wanted to, but because they could not afford a receptionist. However, when they find residence in an incubator, they typically have access to a receptionist who can carry out each of these functions, working for them as well as their fellow residents. Incubator managers use a portion of the revenue collected from the incubator community to pay the salary of the shared receptionist.

Also among the shared resources offered to entrepreneurial residents in a formal business incubator is a variety of office equipment. As is the case with the other shared resources, much of this equipment might be out of the budgetary reach of start-up and early-stage entrepreneurs. However, when their resources are collectively pooled, the incubator is able to afford and provide many of the following types of equipment to share to the incubator community:

- Copy machines
- Fax machines
- Postage machines
- Binding machines
- Shipping scales
- Scanners

Additionally, formal business incubator programs typically tend to offer the following types of products, services and resources to their clients:

- Business plan/market strategy assistance
- Shared receptionist
- Secretarial services
- Phone services (answering service)
- Business resource libraries
- Computer labs
- Computer software
- Common lounging areas
- Business waiting areas
- Audio/visual equipment
- Technical business assistance
- Business services (notary, graphic design, etc.)
- Management consulting
- General business counseling
- Group health insurance
- Technology support services
- Membership in professional organizations, chambers of commerce, or boards of trade
- Business development and financial software
- Manufacturing equipment
- Mentoring/business coaching
- Access to investment capital (angels, venture capital firms)
- "Survival" funding
- Research facilities
- Relocation services
- Interns
- Custodial and maintenance services

Such resource sharing reduces start-up cost barriers for businesses, and it allows them to apply their initial capital and time investment towards building the core business.[25] According to a story featured in the Birmingham Business Journal about incubators, one resident explained, "It's a nurturing environment for a business owner... Starting a business is hard enough without all the other expenses and responsibilities. You can focus on your business, and you don't have to take care of your own bathroom or mop your own floors."[26]

> **Starting a business is hard enough without all the other expenses and responsibilities. You can focus on your business, and you don't have to take care of your own bathroom or mop your own floors.**
>
> **- TENANT IN BIRMINGHAM BUSINESS INCUBATOR**

2. Training Program

No formal business incubator is complete without a training program that is designed to increase the business aptitudes and know-how of its resident entrepreneurs. Every day, thousands of people who are fueled by (what they consider to be) the 'best business idea ever' and a whole heap of passion make the courageous decision to take the huge leap into small business ownership. Before the leap, they were kindergarten teachers, forklift drivers, corporate recruiters, foreign language interpreters, retail salespeople, or even college professors. However, now, they are entrepreneurs. What do they really know about business or running a company? This is where the incubator comes in.

Trained incubator managers understand a critical principle of entrepreneurship that was first popularized by Michael Gerber in *The E-Myth* (a must-read for every new entrepreneur!). According to Gerber, there is a pervasive myth that is accepted by many people, but if accepted by entrepreneurs, it can mean their inevitable demise. The myth: knowing everything there is to know about a particular product or service is the equivalent of knowing what it takes to *run a business* that provides that particular product or service to consumers, Too many times, people who have mastered the development and production of a product or service have ventured out to begin a new enterprise, only to have that enterprise fail within a year or two. It's not that they did not have the passion. It's not that they did not have the product or service knowledge. It's that they did not have the business expertise necessary to properly establish and maintain a business that delivered that product or service.[27]

There is a big difference between knowing how to make or deliver a product or service and knowing how to structure an organization that is able to produce and sell enough of it to a growing customer base in order to produce a sustainable living for the entrepreneur. The product or service itself is simple. It is the start-up organization that drives the production, marketing, sales, and operations of that product or service that is much more complex! This is one of the start-up challenges that makes business incubators necessary. With the proper amount of training, these individuals, who already possess expertise about how to produce a product or deliver a particular service, can actually build viable entrepreneurial organizations to support the production and delivery of their goods to the marketplace, and in turn, earn a sustainable income from them.

Technical Assistance

Some in the incubation world tend to consider training and technical assistance synonymous. However, my research has led me to conclude that there is a clear difference between the two and that they should be offered as separate and distinct incubator services. Training is information that you provide to entrepreneurs on any number of topics that are designed to increase their business proficiency, and consequently, their odds of success. This information not only serves to inform them about what they should know in general about the training topic, but it also helps them understand how they can practically apply the generalities of the topic to their particular venture. Technical assistance, on the other hand, is on-demand expertise that provides additional instruction on how to implement or apply what has already been learned during training sessions. In my professional opinion, it is necessary to differentiate between offering training and offering technical assistance so that business incubator developers will understand the need for having both of these types of information resources available for entrepreneurs.

Regardless of how much training you provide to the entrepreneurs in your incubator program, they will not be equipped with all of the knowledge they need to run a business through these trainings alone. In order to effectively incubate entrepreneurs and their businesses, it will be necessary for you to provide *on-demand* technical assistance. For example, you might provide a training on social media marketing for entrepreneurs, and you might even offer it over the course of a few months, breaking it down into weekly training sessions. However, despite all of the information that they learn in these trainings, when it is time to implement a social media marketing strategy, they will inevitably require additional assistance. Myriad questions are likely to arise as they are engaged in the hands-on process of implementation. When the entrepreneur encounters obstacles along the way or needs to be advised in such technical matters, someone in or affiliated with the incubator should be at their disposal to provide the assistance they need. If an incubator provides lots of training without coupling it with resources that offer such on-demand technical assistance, entrepreneurs are likely to become informed about what to do, but because they do not have day-to-day on-demand help to do what needs to be done, they are likely to become frustrated and stalled in their efforts.

Technical assistance is considered any type of non-monetary assistance that is provided to entrepreneurs that they can access when the need for the assistance arises, or on demand. Ideally, entrepreneurs could attend trainings and grasp everything they ever wanted to know about a particular topic, take the information they learned back to their work spaces, do exactly what they learned in the training, and achieve stellar results without ever having any need of assistance along the way. However, incubators function in the real world, not the ideal world. As entrepreneurs begin to apply what they have learned in their trainings to their businesses, they will need to have some hand holding, gentle guidance, and clarification along the way. Thus, someone should be available to provide such technical assistance, or else, you risk having an incubator full of confused entrepreneurs who could easily move past their obstacles with a little bit of assistance.

It would be ideal for entrepreneurs to be able to walk down the incubator hallway and knock on the door of a full-time incubator staff member who is an expert in all things business in order to receive technical assistance about a particular business process. However, in most cases, when a group is starting out with the development of a new business incubator, the things that are on the "ideal list" take a back seat to the things that the incubator can effectively deliver for now, with plans to deliver more services to its residents in the future when its funding and operations grow. If you are developing a business incubator and discover that having a full-time business expert in residence is not a feasible option at the present time, do not fret! You have many options available to you that will allow you to still be able to provide technical assistance for your entrepreneurs. As with anything in life, the less money you have in the budget, the more creative you must be in order to solve a problem or meet a need.

The individual or team members providing technical assistance to the entrepreneurs do not necessarily need to be housed within your incubator. There are many cases in which an incubator staff is a small one that does not include a technical assistance provider because of budgetary restrictions, space limitations, or both. In such cases, I encourage incubator developers to connect with partners in the community who are willing to provide either free or low cost technical assistance to entrepreneurs who just need a little bit of guidance and help in understanding a particular business process. For example, you might search for Small Business Development Centers (SBDC's) in your area, which are often located on and around college campuses, and ask if they might be willing to partner with you to provide technical assistance to the entrepreneurs in your incubator. They might even be willing to send one of their representatives that has comprehensive knowledge about business to work onsite at the incubator one or two days a week so they can be easily accessible to your incubator residents. You should also consider contacting your local SCORE (Service Corps of Retired Executives) chapter to make the same requests. Known as

"Counselors to America's Small Business," the association is comprised of retired corporate executives who have lots of experience, training and expertise in the types of technical assistance (and mentoring) that will be needed by your entrepreneurs. Best of all, they provide their services for free, so they fall right in line with your budgetary restraints! Never be reluctant to forge alliances and partnerships with others in the community to provide access to services that you cannot provide for entrepreneurs yourself in the business incubator. Incubator developers must necessarily make good use of partnerships and synergies in the community in order to effectively nurture entrepreneurs.

𝑥 .

Access to Networks

If you've ever heard the saying "Relationships make the world go round" and questioned its applicability to the business world, you might need to reconsider! Often, the same is true in business as it is in life: many times, it's not what you know, it's *whom* you know. As an incubator developer, it is essential that you recognize your responsibility to build a network of people in the business world and in the community to advance your incubator's mission, and that you recognize that this is not only your responsibility but the responsibility of everyone who will be working in some significant role of leadership within the business incubator. Prior to developing or working in an incubator, your network of relationships was just for you; it was all about keeping track of who did what, who had the power to do this or that and who knew whom so that if you needed any of them in the future, you could call them and make some things happen based on your relationship with them. However, after developing a business incubator, your networks are no longer just for you; it's time for you to share!

As it has been explained, entrepreneurs who take up residence in your business incubator will probably know a lot about how to produce their product or deliver their service, but they will often know little else of what it takes to be successful in business. Added to this, their knowledge of whom they can contact in business and/or the community to get some things pushed through, have some things decided in their favor, or to get connected with key decision makers is limited. This is where you and the other leaders and mentors in the business incubator come in to save the day!

One of the key benefits of being accepted into a business incubator program is that entrepreneurs know that they will not only have access to space and resources, but they will have access to people who know people... and knowing the right people can be *critical* in business! It is an expectation that as the leader of the incubator, you will utilize *every* key connection, *every* relationship, *every* friendship, *every* person with whom you have influence, *every* friend who knows a friend, and anyone else who has what one of your incubator clients needs in order to help them become successful. This might look like making phone calls on the entrepreneur's behalf, making e-mail introductions between the entrepreneur and a person in your network, or even having a lunch meeting in which you connect the entrepreneur and a key influencer to make a formal introduction. It is up to you to "exploit" your network, not for your own purposes, but for the sake of facilitating the growth, development and success of your incubator clients.

Let's say that you have an entrepreneur who has a landscaping business that specializes in corporate landscaping. Then, let's say that you know someone from your corporate America management days who is the fraternity brother of the regional vice president of a national bank that has several branches housed on large campuses in the area. You talk to your incubator client and let him know that you are planning to find a way to get him connected to a bank that has several large campuses in the area, because if he can land contracts for these corporate campuses, this would represent growth and advancement for his business, not only in terms of revenue but in terms of legitimacy (if his landscaping company does a good job and makes a good impression).

You advise the incubator client to prepare a presentation, proposal and pitch, and you tell him to leave making the connection to you. Then, you put your networking skills to work. First, you set up a call with your friend from corporate America to let him know about your mission to incubate start-ups. Then, you let him know that one of the start-ups in the incubator is a very special company that specializes in corporate landscaping. Next, you ask him if he is still connected to and has any contact with his fraternity brother that is the regional vice president of the bank. If he affirms this, you make the ask: can your friend set up a meeting that includes him, you, and the entrepreneur with the landscaping business? Hopefully, if he understands the give and take of networking relationships, he will agree to try to set it up.

Then, fast forward a month down the line: your friend sets up a lunch meeting that includes the four of you, everyone gets along well, your incubator client makes a brief presentation, hands over a polished, professional proposal (which he received assistance with writing and designing from the incubator staff), and makes the pitch. The regional vice president of the bank wants to do his fraternity brother a favor by supporting your business incubation efforts, so he agrees to give a five-figure contract to your incubator client with a trial run for six months and an option to renew and expand to other campuses based on successful performance during the trial. You have just successfully leveraged your networks for the benefit of an entrepreneur in your incubator!

> *One of the key benefits of being accepted in a business incubator is that entrepreneurs know that they will not only have access to space and resources, but they will have access to people who know people... and knowing the right people is underline critical in business!*

However, while this represents a success for one incubator client, you must now repeat the same process of trying to match the needs of the entrepreneurs in your incubator with what those in your network might be able to offer to meet those needs. Further, this should not be an effort that you alone undertake; *anyone* who works with the incubator, from members of the board of directors (if one exists), to mentors, to advisors and the like should understand that when they bring themselves to the table to support the venture development mission of the incubator, they are also expected to bring their community, business, and professional networks and contacts to the table with them, leveraging them in *any* way possible to nurture the success of the incubator's entrepreneurs. Access to networks is simply giving entrepreneurs inroads into the relationships you have with others so they can use them for their own purposes, because businesses are built on relationships, and you are in the business of growing businesses!

5. Coaching/Mentoring

There's no such thing as someone who does not need a coach. Show me someone who is successful at what they do, and I will show you someone who has been coached somewhere along the way. As successful as NBA basketball players Michael Jordan and Kobe Bryant were, they had coaches from the time they dressed out for their very first practice until the days they retired. As amazing a golfer as Tiger Woods was, even as a prodigious child, he had to have a coach to become a professional golfer and to achieve the tremendous success that he did in the PGA. As superhuman as Olympic swimmer Michael Phelps seems, he is the most decorated Olympian of all time because he had a swim coach from the time he was a young child all the way through his Olympic career. Simply put, it takes coaching to *become* successful, and it takes coaching to *stay* successful!

If you will nurture successful entrepreneurs in your incubator, you must provide access to coaching for them. It's a good idea to pair your incubator clients with a coach when they are in their start-up infancy so that they develop good habits, specifically, the ability to receive coaching from others who can help them take their business to the next level. If they learn this early on in the initial stages of their business development, they will be much more likely to be coachable when their entrepreneurial venture begins to grow and realize some success. This is important to consider, primarily because once incubator clients grow their businesses to the point at which they consider themselves successful (a definition which varies from entrepreneur to entrepreneur because it is up to each entrepreneur to define his or her own notion of success), the potential exists that they will begin to become resistant to external counsel. In their minds, they started their business from the ground up knowing nothing about business, and they relied upon a combination of heart, hard work, long hours, determination and gut feelings to produce the "successful" business they currently have, so they do not feel the need to listen to what anyone else has to say about how to build a successful enterprise. Rather than sit down and listen to a seasoned veteran of a coach counsel them on how to take their business to the next level, they feel like they themselves should be writing a book on how to get it done! This is a posture that could potentially lead to a short life span for a business, because becoming successful is one thing; maintaining that success is quite another.

Far too often, entrepreneurs, especially those who have tasted some measure of what they consider to be success, are closed to receiving coaching and mentoring from others. They might adopt such a position for several reasons. Perhaps they feel that someone who is an outsider and who knows nothing about them and what they have done to build the venture to its current state of success is not qualified to coach to them about their business, because they are the only ones on the planet who know their business intimately. Perhaps they feel that if they listen to an outsider provide mentoring and counseling to them about their business and things go wrong, they will regret not relying upon their own wisdom and intuition concerning the business they have built. Another reason might be pride: they do not want to receive any type of counseling or mentoring from an industry veteran or business expert because if their business becomes the success that they believe it will be, they want to be able to take the full credit for its development rather than having to share the glory with someone else. They want to be the "self-made" entrepreneur, not the "group-made" entrepreneur. Finally, there's the reason that makes people in any area of life un-coachable and unwilling to receive the wisdom of a sage mentor: they believe that they already know all of the answers, so additional input is not necessary, thank you very much!

Knowing that there are people who are prone to be possessive, fearful, rugged individualists who are greedy for independent glory, and therefore resistant to mentoring and coaching, and knowing that mentoring and coaching are critical to becoming successful and staying successful (just ask any champion who has ever lived!), it is incumbent upon the incubator management to develop a culture in which mentoring and coaching are prized, valued and considered of utmost importance in the formula for any business to become a success. This culture must be cultivated by everyone operating in a position of leadership in the incubator. Otherwise, providing coaching and mentoring as a service that is designed to nurture the entrepreneurs and help their businesses to grow, thrive and survive will be an exercise in futility. You will have lots of coaches and mentors on hand, but they will be simply twiddling their thumbs because none of the entrepreneurs will seem to be in need of their services.

Coaching and mentoring, in regards to incubator clients, can be used interchangeably. The concept simply entails someone with a respectable level of business knowledge and experience gaining an understanding of the incubator client's business goals, particularly where the client envisions the business will be at a certain point in the future, and then providing the client with advice, guidance, and expert wisdom on how to reach these goals. If the incubator client is not clear on these goals, the incubator's coaches and mentors should help the client to establish them for the business so that together, the client and mentor or coach can work towards manifesting them. As a part of this process, a coach or mentor will keep entrepreneurs accountable to the attainment of their goals and help to refocus or redirect them when they stray off course or find themselves off-task, which is easy to do when you are a hungry entrepreneur chasing success. A good coach or mentor will help an incubator client work smarter rather than harder, sharing business concepts, examples of real-life personal experiences, knowledge about what other businesses have done that have lessons applicable to the entrepreneur's current stage of growth, motivation and encouragement, and anything else that he or she deems necessary to help nurture the entrepreneur in the development of the start-up venture.

After cultivating a culture of coachability among incubator clients, incubator managers should identify and assign each and every entrepreneur in the incubator to a hand-selected coach or mentor that the manager deems to be a good fit for the needs of both the incubator client and his or her type and stage of business. These coaches and mentors should not be inexperienced, "fly-by-night" individuals who have extra time on their hands to offer some subjective opinions to new start-ups. Instead, they should be qualified for the task at hand through years of training and by having had first-hand experience in the business world or with start-up ventures. In most incubators, coaches and mentors tend to be corporate executives, industry leaders, community influencers and other successful entrepreneurs who are looking to share what they have learned with those who are new to the entrepreneurial community.

A Champion

An incubator champion is the incubator president, director or manager of the organization – the very *heartbeat* of the incubator. In my research-based estimation, this individual, or "champion" as I prefer to call him or her, is the key to any incubator's effectiveness in nurturing and graduating entrepreneurs. This is the individual who oversees all of the operations, and the training, development and growth systems of the business incubator, the person who has a thumb on the pulse of every business in the incubator, and the person who is, by far, the biggest advocate for the incubator clients in the entire organization!

The more you learn about the development of business incubators, the more you will realize one thing to be true: a business incubator is a *business*! Any person who begins a start-up business must be a self-starting, self-motivated entrepreneur with vision, drive, expertise, resilience, and most of all, passion. Entrepreneurs must be their own biggest champions for their business, helping to start it, advance it, keep it going, fight for it, promote it, advocate for it, and support it with all they've got; no one else is going to do it for them! These are the same traits that should characterize an incubator champion, with one difference: the average entrepreneur has to build and fight for only one business... his or her own. The incubator champion, as an entrepreneur (who runs an incubator business), must fight for *every* business in the incubator! It is for this reason that no other individual in the incubator should be a bigger advocate for the businesses in the incubator than the incubator president, director, or manager.

I liken the individual who performs this role in the incubator to that of a mother hen who incubates her eggs. She knows them better than anyone else, is fiercely protective of them, provides all of the support and nurture that they need to hatch and grow and develop into healthy little chickens that can live independently on their own, and will use every resource within her power to ensure that they succeed in life. Just as a mother hen is committed to incubating and nurturing her eggs until they can survive without her, so an incubator champion is committed to incubating and nurturing businesses that can be birthed, grow, thrive and survive on their own!

A Snapshot of Business Incubation in the U.S.

It is very difficult to determine an official number of incubators in existence in the United States at any given time. The best estimates for approximating how many of these organizations exist in the U.S. can be based on the North American members that belong to the International Business Innovation Association (InBIA). In 2017, the InBIA reported that it had more than 1,900 incubator clients in over 60 nations, comprised of incubator managers and developers as well as groups and individuals who are interested in business incubation. Seventy-five percent of these members were in North America, while 25 percent of its members were from other nations.[28] Based on these percentages, it can be estimated that there are approximately 1,400 business incubators in the United States.

The InBIA classifies the formal incubators that comprise their membership into five different types:

- Academic institutions
- Nonprofit development corporations
- For-profit property development ventures
- Venture capital firms
- A combination of more than one type[29]

Practical facts surrounding business incubators are quite interesting. According to the InBIA's 2012 State of the Business Incubation Industry report:[30]

- The average business incubator has been in operation for about 12 years. Some incubators have been open and incubating businesses for more than 20 years.

- The average business incubator facility is 32,319 square feet, which is approximately 5,000 square feet lower than facility sizes reported in 2006.

- The average incubator occupancy is 74%. Although more incubators are introducing virtual incubation, 93% of business incubators had an actual physical facility in which they house and incubate their clients.

- The average number of companies that incubators served as resident and affiliate clients was 35, an all-time high in the history of incubator research.

- The average number of resident clients that incubators served was 20, and the average number of affiliate clients served was 15, both increases over numbers reported in the past.

- Resident clients who graduated from incubator programs received full incubation services for an average of 28 months, less time than the average of 33 months that was reported only six years earlier in 2006. Virtual or affiliate clients received incubator services for an average of 19 months before graduating.

- In North America, 54% of business incubators are mixed-use, meaning they serve a variety of types of businesses rather than targeting a specific industry sector.

- Incubators that target specific industry sectors tended to focus on information technology, computer software, biosciences/life science, energy and the environment.

- Incubators that target specific demographic groups tended

to target micro-entrepreneurs, college and university students, Hispanics, women and African-Americans.

The Clear and Present Demand for
Business Incubators

Once the true concept of business incubation is clearly explained to individuals who were previously ignorant of the idea, they tend to immediately grab onto the concept as a wonderful, even logical initiative! If you take things a step further and begin to brag on the highly-impressive business incubation statistics (that 87-90% of incubated small businesses are still open after 5 years as compared with only 20% of non-incubated businesses), their immediate reply is often much like mine was when I first learned of the effectiveness of business incubation: "Wow! Why don't *all* start-ups use business incubators?"

Business incubators are slowly but steadily gaining notoriety across the U.S. and the shores beyond as an effective, innovative and entrepreneurial development tool. In fact, they are becoming more popular and sought out by entrepreneurs who have heard of their existence, as many early-stage, fledgling and would-be business owners regard formal incubators as just the resource that they need in order to succeed in the long-term. Even still, while there are some who possess the knowledge that incubators exist, exactly what they do and what they have to offer is often unknown. Once the public is informed and educated about business incubators, it is not difficult to sell them on the idea that these relatively unknown resources offer major advantages for small business development.

In 1998, a study was conducted on business incubation by the University of Michigan, the National Business Incubation Association (NBIA), Ohio University and the Southern Technology Council under a grant from the U.S. Department of Commerce Economic Development Administration. It was groundbreaking at the time, as it was the largest scientific study to be conducted on the incubator industry after a surge of incubator development occurred in North America. Dinah Adkins, former President and CEO of the NBIA, commented about the study, stating the following: "Business incubation programs treat entrepreneurial companies as important community and national resources and provide assistance that ensures a company's success. This study should convince communities that if they don't already have a business incubation program, they'll want to start thinking about one."[31] Prior to this research study, there had only been anecdotal information that suggested that business incubation could be utilized as a successful economic development strategy. The clear demand was present for business incubators at that time, and the demand for business incubation services and the support and resources they offer only continues to grow.

Business Accelerators vs. Business Incubators

If you've been following the business development industry for any amount of time, you have no doubt heard the term business "incubator" tossed around in the same conversation as the term business "accelerator." The lack of general understanding about what the two terms mean has led to some business development programs that are actually accelerators labeling themselves as "incubators," and other programs that are, in fact, incubators referring to themselves as "accelerators." However, the two are not synonymous, and the terms should *not* be used interchangeably. Although accelerators are considered to be close cousins to business incubators, their nature and function call for us to resist equating them with business incubators.

The fact that there are some variations on each of these types of entrepreneurial support programs makes the lines of differentiation between them a little fuzzy. Generally speaking, both incubators and accelerators are driven by a mission of helping start-up and early-stage companies survive the critical early stages of life. Both incubators and accelerators provide entrepreneurs with education, coaching, technical assistance, and the resources they need in order to grow, develop and become viable, able to stand on their own. However, incubators and accelerators differ in terms of who leads them, the types of companies permitted entry into them and the stakes for being accepted into them.

Business incubators are typically established and primarily funded by nonprofit entities like economic development organizations, civic associations, city government agencies, and academic institutions that are seeking to develop businesses with a mission of spurring economic development, job creation and an entrepreneurial climate in their local territory. Unless they specify that they are targeted to start-ups in a particular industry (software, food, multimedia, the arts, etc.), most all nonprofit business incubators allow entry to just about any type of start-up business with high-growth potential. When approved for residence in the incubator, entrepreneurs pay below-market rent and have full access to the incubator resources during their residency, which can span anywhere from one year to several years, as the amount of time that an incubator resident will spend in an incubator will vary from start-up to start-up. Businesses do not graduate or spin out of the incubator until they are stable, profitable and viable, a level of maturity that is not reached overnight. However, the entrepreneurs typically maintain full ownership of their business in a nonprofit business incubator. (Note: Although unlikely that incubators will take equity, the NBIA reports that a small percentage – 18 percent – of incubators take equity in all or some of their client companies, and as expected, the likelihood of taking equity is higher in for-profit incubators with tech clients).[32] Overall, nonprofit business incubators are focused on building strong businesses, knowing that strong businesses build strong communities through economic development, taxation, job creation, and revenue invested back to the community, among other notable benefits. Thus, nonprofit business incubators aim to nurture a start-up or early-stage business' growth to the point that it is viable, sustainable and can stand on its own, recognizing that their investment in these businesses are investments in their own community.

Accelerators, on the other hand, tend to be established and funded by investment firms that are seeking an opportunity to make lots of money off of the next big business idea. For this reason, rather than allow entry to any business in any industry with high-growth potential, they tend to almost exclusively target technology companies to fill the space in their organizations, as this is a high-stakes, high-profit industry that can result in the making of multi-millionaires, seemingly in the blink of an eye. With the right amount of capital infusion and the proper guidance and direction from experienced technology veterans, if they get their hands on the right entrepreneur with the right idea, they can stand to make a *huge* profit! However, unlike a nonprofit business incubator, when the business thrives in a business accelerator, the entrepreneur does not profit alone; the accelerator's managers also profit. In order to gain residence and access to the resources in a business accelerator, a business, which is typically a more developed, early-stage venture, must generally give up *at least* a 6% equity stake (ownership percentage) in the business in exchange for partaking of the benefits of participation in the accelerator program.

To be fair, while requiring an equity stake in the businesses they work with, accelerators make a great deal of investment in the ventures they support, from offering them ample cash, to free office space and access to the most current, cutting-edge technology and resources that entrepreneurs can use to develop their ideas.

Being granted entry into the right accelerator can have some real advantages for the entrepreneur. For example, venture capitalists, which are groups of private investors who buy equity in high-risk (typically tech) start-ups at a discount and provide the critical access to capital that these companies need to thrive, are more likely to invest millions of dollars into entrepreneurs for the development and growth of their start-ups when these start-ups are housed in a prominent business accelerator that is known for producing successful tech companies.

> *Although many people outside the industry use the terms "incubator" and "accelerator" interchangeably, most of these seed accelerators are not true incubation programs in the typical sense. Instead, they operate as for-profits designed to bring a return on investment to their sponsors by providing fast-test validation of business ideas, typically in fields such as mobile applications, gaming and related areas.*
>
> — LINDA KNOPP,
> NATIONAL BUSINESS INCUBATION ASSOCIATION

Also, the level of expertise that tech business accelerators offer to their residents, typically expert guidance from technology hotshots with proven abilities to take a tech idea from zero to a must-have global sensation almost overnight, also tends to be top-shelf and in high demand. Together, the mentors, executive coaches, technology gurus, support personnel and the start-up entrepreneur work together to generate funding from venture capitalists, develop the idea, test it, tweak it, introduce it to the market, and make a ton of profit – and *quickly*! The profit is split between the start-up, the accelerator, the venture capitalists, and anyone else who has negotiated an equity stake in the business in exchange for helping it to grow and become profitable. In the world of business accelerators, the aim is clear: make as much money as possible as quickly as possible. The tech world changes and develops at the speed of thought; what was relevant and popular today can be on its way to obsolete tomorrow. It is for this reason that while a start-up can remain in a nonprofit incubator for years before spinning out into its own facilities, a start-up might remain in an accelerator for only three to six months. The time from idea to market for a tech start-up is a quick one, especially when it is facilitated by the ready access to capital and expert knowledge that a business accelerator offers.

Business accelerator programs also typically work with larger numbers of entrepreneurs than nonprofit business incubators. Nonprofit business incubators will work with as many start-up clients as their space will allow, and because of their restricted budgets and space considerations, these numbers are usually limited. They must also consider how many start-ups they can effectively serve with their network of mentors, coaches and support personnel and restrict the number of residents allowed entry into their incubators accordingly. However, with an abundance of capital resources and facility spaces that are constructed to house larger numbers of start-ups, networks of private investors vying to give money to the next big start-up idea, executives and technology professionals flooding their offices with requests to work with their residents, and the ability to pay larger support staff members, business accelerators might work with scores of start-ups at one time. This leads to cycling cohorts of start-ups in and out of the intense accelerator program as their ideas are developed – or worse, as they become obsolete or irrelevant during the process of development. They generally graduate from the accelerator when they have completed the accelerator's training program whether the start-up is stable and viable or not (unlike nonprofit business incubators).

Only a few of the tech companies that go through the accelerator's training and development program might be allowed to remain as residents in the accelerator and be managed as a part of the accelerator's portfolio, because they show a great deal of growth and profit potential. This is another reason for the large numbers of start-ups that are granted entry into business accelerators: business accelerator managers are realistic about the state of tech start-ups and know that only one to two percent of the companies with which they work might actually become big hits in the mass market. However, the profit that they earn from these start-up giants will more than offset the investments that they have made in the myriad other start-ups in the accelerator that fail to catch on and become the successes that the accelerator thought they might be.

All said, both nonprofit business incubators and for-profit business accelerators have the same basic mission with different methods and motivations. Nonprofit business incubators nurture and support start-ups because they know that strong businesses build strong communities, and their mission is typically to build a stronger community by economically developing it through entrepreneurship. For-profit business accelerators nurture and support start-ups because they want to make money. Nonprofit business incubators are driven to support a start-up until it can stand and survive on its own, just as a mother hen will incubate her chicks until they are viable. Business accelerators are limited-duration programs that are driven to quickly train, counsel and test groups of tech start-ups, fast-tracking them to the market, graduating them or spinning them out whether they are fully viable or not. The pages of this book focus on establishing nonprofit business incubators, as I believe that they are more beneficial for the development of stable, sustainable entrepreneurial ventures and stronger local economies. Is start-up survival a guarantee if a business is incubated? Of course, not. However, businesses that are incubated in a nonprofit business incubator have a significantly higher success rate than those who do not receive such support.

Formal or Residential Business
Incubator Programs

There are currently 1,400 formal business incubators in operation in North America (up from 1,100 in 2006) that offer residence to entrepreneurs.[33] A formal or resident business incubator is designed to provide a nurturing environment for start-up or existing businesses to grow and develop, and it often houses its operations within a dedicated facility that makes space available for entrepreneurs to house their businesses for a fee. This aspect of incubation is what differentiates the formal from the virtual or affiliate business incubator programs the most. Formal or residential incubator programs typically provide office or production space, business and technical assistance, and support services that increase the likelihood of survival for the small business to entrepreneurs whose businesses are located within the physical space of the incubator.[34]

Among formal or residential business incubator programs, incubators may be either for-profit or nonprofit organizations. Keep in mind, however, that just because a business incubator is classified as nonprofit, this does not mean that the organization will not make a profit, for every organization needs to generate profit in order to sustain its operations and grow.

For-profit Business Incubators

For-profit business incubators are most often privately-owned and profit from the development of the profitable enterprises housed in their incubators. It is not an uncommon practice for for-profit incubators to receive equity in exchange for allowing businesses to occupy space in their incubator and access to their resources, though these types of for-profit incubators comprise only 7% of all incubators.[35]

Nonprofit Business Incubators

Nonprofit business incubators may be either public or private and are often driven by an agenda of development. These organizations are most often sponsored by nonprofit economic development organizations or local government agencies and have job creation, economic development or other government-related goals as their core mission.[36] These may also be academic incubators, which are usually formed by a college, university or other academic institution in collaboration with representatives from private industry, or a hybrid of one or more forms of nonprofit incubators. In 2012, 32% of incubator programs were sponsored by two-year or four-year colleges or universities, the highest percentage reported in research since 1989.[37]

Finally, a hybrid incubator usually combines characteristics of any of the incubator types in any particular fashion.[38] Nonprofit incubators make up 93% of incubators in North America and are often partnerships with nonprofit organizations, community development programs, and other groups or private businesses with an interest in business development.

Virtual or Affiliate Incubator Programs

Although 93 percent of incubation programs have a physical facility in which they house and incubate their clients,[39] virtual and affiliate programs are increasing in popularity. Aside from services offered to formal business incubator clients, many incubators offer services to the community either free of charge, on a fee-per-service basis, or on a flat membership fee. These types of programs are often referred to within the incubator industry as "virtual incubators," "affiliates," or "incubators without walls," because they offer a variety of services to incubate businesses without providing actual residential space within the incubator. A study conducted by the NBIA showed that more than half of all business incubation programs served clients virtually or as affiliates who utilized the incubator's programming, mentoring and technical services without being physically housed in the incubator.[40]

An entrepreneur might participate as a virtual or affiliate member of a business incubator for a number of reasons. For example, the incubator might be filled to capacity with other start-ups, and there is no physical space within the incubator to house new start-ups until some of the existing start-ups graduate from the program. Other entrepreneurs might be happy with their current workspaces outside of the incubator but would like to have access to the mentorship, skills training, and technical support that the virtual or affiliate program can offer them without being housed in the facility. Some entrepreneurs might not meet all of the criteria required for residence in the incubator but have a feasible business plan and enough growth potential for the incubator program to work with them virtually. Then, there are other entrepreneurs who might live too far away from the incubator to house their businesses in it; their remote location calls for them to access the incubator programs and services virtually.

Virtual incubator services offered by both formal and informal incubation programs are usually open to any business owner in the community, and some incubation programs even require participation in this type of program a prerequisite to becoming a resident in the incubator. These programs often offer a combination of virtual support and in-person workshops to their affiliate members on how to write business plans, marketing on a budget, credit counseling, how to qualify for a loan, how to build a basic website, networking, the basics of business budgeting, negotiating, and insurance, among other topics of interest to the existing or aspiring entrepreneur. While these programs may be presented by the staff members of the incubator, they may also utilize guest professionals from the community who volunteer to make such beneficial presentations free of charge to attendees.

Additionally, these informal or virtual incubator programs may extend to offering the benefits of participating in their access-to-capital or loan programs to non-resident members of the community. For example, the Wisconsin Women's Business Initiative Corporation charges a fee of $75 to business owners to become a member of their lending program, and this fee is placed into a loan loss reserve fund.[41] In addition to allowing people in the community to participate in their loan programs, informal and virtual incubators may allow participation in brown-bag forums, seminars and trainings, technical assistance programs, mentoring programs or consulting sessions. It is not unusual for this type of virtual incubator program to receive public funding to supplement the program expenses that accompany the provision of these services.

3

The Benefits of Business Incubation

Reducing Risk & Boosting Survival through Space, Support & Synergy

Whenever I embark upon a discussion of the bountiful benefits of business incubation, I like to utilize a story that helps to create a word picture in the imagination. This tale is about an early-stage business owner, his entrepreneurial challenge, and the decisions that would determine his destiny. Allow me to introduce to you "Lester's Story" presented from two accounts: The Incubated Version and The Non-Incubated Version.

Lester's Story: The Incubated Version

Lester was really struggling as an entrepreneur. He had left his job as a social worker six months prior to pursue his dream of starting his own business, and he was confident that the employee drug screening services that he was offering were well-needed in the big city in which he lived. After all, only one other company in the city offered the service, but he felt he had an advantage over them: his cost was 25% less for the exact same service, his results turnaround time was 50% faster, and he was mobile in providing his services – his one competitor was not. However, Lester was working out of his home and needed professional office space for client companies that wanted to send their existing and prospective employees for screening.

Lester's clientele base was very small because he had no money for developing marketing materials and no money for placing ads in local media. In fact, he had no money for anything, because the little profit that he received from his mobile drug screening work only barely paid for the gas in the car and the bills. After all expenses and bills were paid, there was never any salary left over for him, even though some days, he worked 12 to 14 hours straight. This was not the world of business ownership that he'd imagined. To make matters worse, Lester had gone to a city government bid fair where the city in which he lived offered contract opportunities to qualified small businesses. The good news is that Lester had won a huge contract with the city to screen all 17 of its departments' employees, but the bad news is that Lester felt completely overwhelmed, in over his head, and did not know where to begin. He did not use formal accounting software to manage his finances, only a spiral notebook and a basic checking account. He was not really administrative, and he kept up with his appointments and clients out of the same spiral notebook where he tracked his payments. Lester only had 4 months until the city's contract took effect before he had to start providing the services – or lose the contract, and potentially lose his business. He felt lost. What was Lester to do?

One day, Lester, tired from a long day's work, attended a networking reception for small business owners. He went to these types of events often because they were great for meeting potential clients. Midway through the event, the reception's sponsor came to the podium and had a few words. Lester listened attentively. The polished lady in the business suit who spoke introduced herself as the director of a local business incubator. *A business incubator?* Lester thought. What's that? After the lady explained what a business incubator was and how they could help early-stage businesses grow, Lester's interest was piqued. He realized he needed help if his business was going to survive, and he wasn't too proud to ask for assistance. He was proud of his own courage for launching out to start the business, and he was also proud of the work that he had done so far to build his clientele, but Lester realized that without some intervention, he simply could not continue to keep the business open at this rate.

Lester picked up the lady's card at the reception, and within one week, he had filled out an application at the business incubator and submitted a copy of his business plan. A couple of weeks after that, he had an interview with several members of the incubator's screening board, and within several weeks of seeing the young lady's presentation at the networking reception, Lester was moving his business into the business incubator!

Lester's office space was nice. *Really* nice. He had a small professional suite that housed three offices and one supply storage area, and the rent that he was paying for the space was less than any commercial space he'd ever seen! Furthermore, the offices were fully furnished with desks, executive chairs, file cabinets, telephones and active internet lines. There was even one laptop computer on his desk that the incubator loaned him. At the close of move-in day, Lester had to attend an incubator orientation that reviewed all of the requirements of incubator residency. A couple of days after Lester moved in, he met with the power team that the incubator had assembled just for him: a group of high-power, influential, well-connected business owners and corporate executives in the community that donated their time to mentoring young businesses. They asked him about where he was with his business and what he needed. With every challenge that Lester introduced, one of his power team members would tell him who to contact, what to ask for, and what to expect – and they would follow this expert advice with, "And tell him I sent you. He'll take care of you." Lester was amazed. All of the answers to his questions in one room! Expert advice and personal connections provided freely! If he had not experienced it himself, he would not have believed it.

Things only went uphill from there. By the end of the week, the incubator had introduced Lester to its in-house design team which was now working on professional marketing materials and advertisements for Lester's business. The incubator had an arrangement for low-cost printing with a local printer and would bill Lester for the expense later. The incubator also had an arrangement with several local newspapers for low-cost ad space for its incubator residents, so pretty soon, Lester's business was in the newspaper too. At a lunch meeting, the incubator capital coordinator introduced Lester to a local angel investor that had an interest in funding the small business dreams of others. On a handshake, he committed to funding Lester's business to the tune of $25,000, and he would require that Lester only pay back $5,000 after one year.

The incubator manager gave Lester access to the incubator's administrative talent pool, which included resumes of various individuals in the community interested in working with early-stage businesses. Lester interviewed four candidates and ended up hiring two of them at very reasonable rates: one individual with 10 years of sales and administrative experience and the other with seven years of small business accounting experience and 10 years of IT (information technology) experience. After having a meeting with his new staffers, the incubator's finance coordinator, and the incubator's marketing assistance coordinator, Lester's books were completely in order in only five days, his website was virtually complete, and his business was able to book appointments online – with the option of coming in to his new professional office for screenings.

The phone was ringing off the hook from all of the attention the business was receiving from marketing... except now, Lester did not have to answer it. His administrative assistants did. Lester's business was now on the fast-track to success. Within three years, he outgrew his space in the incubator, moved into his own large facility, and today, his company is the city's leading provider of drug screening services. Lester now pays it forward by serving on the power teams for two other businesses housed in the incubator.

Lester's Story – The Non-Incubated Version

Unfortunately, in this version of the story, Lester's story ended the day he was introduced to the business incubation representative at the networking reception. Instead of following up on the assistance that the business incubator offered, he decided to go it alone – after all, he thought, no one would actually give him all of that help for free, right? Within two months, Lester was looking for a job again to supplement the lack of income he was facing in the business. His pledge to himself was that this job was only temporary, and he would still keep doing his drug screening business on the side. Within one month after working at his job, the business was simply too much to keep up with; so, like 80% of the other entrepreneurs that start businesses, Lester closed his doors on his dream. He is now back to working as a social worker with long hours, little pay, and a heavy heart that mourns the loss of the business that could have been.

> In fact, statistics show that 87% to 90% of all businesses that graduate out of incubator programs are still in business. This is contrasted with approximately 20% to 30% of non-incubated businesses that are still in business after the same length of time.

Bottom Line Benefits: Incubators Reduce the Risk of Failure & Boost Business Survival Rates!

After reading a story like Lester's, what small business owner wouldn't want to house their business in a business incubator? Now, I understand Lester's thought that there is simply no way that any organization would give this type of help away for free. Even I, upon hearing about the vast benefits that incubators provide, was compelled to ask, "What's the catch?" When dealing with nonprofit incubators, there is no catch. Remember, it is the for-profit incubator industry that will normally require equity in the start-up, repayment of loans with higher interest, and someone whom the incubator management chooses to lead and make critical decisions for the business. Even then,

I would not call these for-profit incubator characteristics a "catch" so much as I would simply call them "different requirements for incubator residency."

Conversely, nonprofit business incubators are usually funded by local and federal grants, private foundations and resident rents, so there is no need to require their residents to give up an arm and a leg or even a part of their business in exchange for the benefits the incubator offers. Further, these incubators are normally run by people like me: those driven by a passion for helping to develop small businesses, not those driven by money (of course, there is a salary involved that increases with the success of the incubator, but this is not the motivating factor).

It is important for those who will establish business incubators to be clear on the benefits of business incubation, because it will be necessary to transfer this enthusiasm to small business owners who might be skeptical about receiving such assistance. Concerning the benefits of incubator residency, the facts are clear: formal business incubation significantly increases the chances of survival for businesses. Lester's story is quite typical of what an early-stage business can expect to receive in a good, functional business incubator.

There is no denying the statistical evidence surrounding the success of business incubation. According to the InBIA, business incubators reduce the risk of small business failures.[42] In fact, statistics show that 87% to 90% of all businesses that graduate out of incubator programs are still in business. This is contrasted with approximately 20% to 30% of non-incubated businesses that are still in business after the same length of time. The effects of taking up residence in a business incubator also reach into the revenue stream of businesses, as the average firm's sales increase by more than 400% from the time it enters until the time it leaves the incubator and as start-up firms in incubators annually increased sales by $240,000 each and added an average of 3.7 full- and part-time jobs per firm.[43]

While incubator researchers tout the high survival rates of incubated start-ups relative to non-incubated businesses, I feel a responsibility to address a concern of some who question whether the success rates of incubated businesses can be legitimately compared against the success rates of non-incubated businesses, because incubators only allow entry to and provide support for businesses that they hand select based on their critical evaluation of the start-up's potential for high growth and viability.[44] I would say that these individuals are focused on the wrong issue; they should be focused on the idea that there are potentially high-growth and successful businesses, both within incubators and outside of incubators. However, we have solid research results that show that when start-up businesses are incubated and provided with access to the support and resources of an incubator, they are significantly more likely to become viable and succeed rather than close their doors like the majority of non-incubated business.

Offering Value to Entrepreneurs: What's In It for Incubator Clients?

Contrary to many examples of so-called business incubator programs that exist, a formal incubator program is more than just a renovated, previously-abandoned building that offers cheap space to start-ups. If a start-up or existing business owner is fortunate enough to be granted entry into an incubator organization, he or she is granted access to a world of amenities, benefits and resources that will assist in the effective nurturing and development of the small business. Essentially, these programs offer a one-stop-shopping concept in which there are numerous products and resources all conveniently and efficiently co-located under one roof for the benefit of the entrepreneur—and all for one low cost.

The ability to locate a business in an incubator is also beneficial because most incubators allow businesses to sign short-term, flexible leases in which the business occupies only the smallest amount of space that is needed for the business. As the business expands, it is conveniently allowed to move to a larger space in the incubator as many times as necessary to accommodate the business' growth. Thus, the businesses only pay for what they need at any stage of growth, allowing their overhead costs to keep scale with their revenues. Rents are usually below market rate, often in the range of 20%-30% below.

Incubator residents are also granted the convenience of having on-site technical assistance and business counseling, because business owners might not know what questions to ask or to whom they can ask them concerning a particular matter. This is essential, because although many small business owners know how to perform the technical functions to produce their product or service, many do not know the first thing about running a small business (or in many cases, what they do know is erroneous). Incubator staff members recognize that they exist to ensure the success of their resident small businesses, and because of this, staff members tend to have open door policies offering "doorway consulting" in which they can lend their expert advice to the business owner one-on-one. Practically speaking, each member of the incubator staff is a small business consultant. Such managerial or financial consulting may be scheduled sit-down sessions to help business owners reach long-term projected goals, or they may be on-the-spot, as it is sometimes necessary to put out fires that might flare up in the business. According to Garrity, "This is the true core of what an incubator provides and often can help fill in gaps in skills of new businesses."[45]

While incubator managers and their staff often provide these services to the incubator residents, many of the resources and services that are made available to the incubator residents are offered through networks that the incubator has formed with community professionals, local community colleges and universities, nonprofit community organizations, and private corporations who desire to invest in small business growth and development in their local community. Professionals that will offer their services to residents pro-bono, or for a reduced fee, include lawyers, accountants, bankers, and consultants, and advertising experts. These individuals are usually utilized for seminar presentations or mentoring incubator clients. Most incubators compile a thorough listing of the resources available either within the walls of the incubator or through contacts in the community, but if new needs arise that cannot be met by existing resources or contacts, additional contacts and networks are developed to effectively address the need of the incubator client. Thus, under good management, the list of available resources in a business incubator tends to be in a dynamic state of expansion at all times.

Table 1 details some of the resources and services available to incubator residents that fall into three categories: shared office, management/technical assistance, and financing.

Table 1. Resources and Services for Incubator Residents[46]

Shared Office	Management/Technical Assistance	Financing
Conference room	Business plans	Externally aided
Photocopying	Marketing	Internally provided
Receptionist coverage	Accounting	
Word processing/typist	Government grants and loans	
Security	Legal services	
Computer equipment	Patent assistance	
Fax machine	Computer training	
Office equipment/furniture	International trade	
Business library	Government procurement	
Audio/visual equipment	Equity and debt financing	
Extra storage	Access to sophisticated computer processing	
Bookkeeping	Access to other resources outside the incubator	
Group health insurance	Research and development	
	Business tax assistance	

While access to each of the services and resources listed plays an invaluable role in the entrepreneur's business success, respondents in one incubator research study that represented the resident enterprises considered the atmosphere and moral support the most important provision in the incubator.[47]

One of the most critical pieces of advice that I have ever received about life as an entrepreneur came from my professor and mentor at The University of Texas at Austin, Dr. John Sibley Butler. During one of his inspirational and informative lectures, he once said, "Whatever you do, if you are an entrepreneur and want to survive, you must surround yourself with other entrepreneurs. Put yourself in an entrepreneurial environment! This is critical to your ability to weather the challenges of entrepreneurship, remain motivated on the entrepreneurial rollercoaster, and build a successful start-up." I remember that when I heard him say this, it really stood out to me. I wrote it down on my notepad and highlighted it for emphasis, because even though I was not actively engaged in my own entrepreneurial endeavor, he was so adamant about the idea that I knew it deserved my attention. Not many years later, when I began my first venture, I got it.

Dr. Butler understood the valuable synergy that is created when entrepreneurs are placed within the same context. The business dictionary definition of synergy is:

A state in which two or more things work together in a particularly fruitful way that produces an effect greater than the sum of their individual effects. Expressed also as "the whole is greater than the sum of the parts."[48]

When business incubators bring entrepreneurs and their start-up enterprises under one roof to nurture and develop them to viability, the arrangement is one that has widespread benefits for everyone involved. The types of encouragement in the incubator environment, the opportunity to be surrounded by other business owners who are also in their fledgling stages, and the internal security of having a support system that is working to ensure the success of one's business, are unique to formal incubator environments, and these elements make incubators the desired choice for many entrepreneurs. Incubator residents enjoy the sense of community, encouragement, camaraderie and moral support that they experience within incubator walls as fledgling entrepreneurs. There are some notable benefits of the synergy that is created as a result of an entrepreneur's residence in a business incubator.

> *If you are an entrepreneur and want to survive, you must surround yourself with other entrepreneurs. Place yourself in an entrepreneurial environment! This is <u>critical</u> to your ability to weather the challenges of entrepreneurship, remain motivated on the entrepreneurial rollercoaster...*
>
> **- DR. JOHN SIBLEY BUTLER,**
> **THE UNIVERSITY OF TEXAS AT AUSTIN**

For example, one of these significant benefits is that residence in a business incubator combats entrepreneurial isolation through the establishment of community. When residing in a business incubator, entrepreneurs are surrounded by individuals just like them who are engaged in the same struggles of early-stage entrepreneurship. Life can be very lonely for an entrepreneur, because most people begin their entrepreneurial journey as solopreneurs, working all alone. Incubators provide not only access to resources and support but access to other men and women who are a part of an entrepreneurial community.

Being a part of an entrepreneurial community is essential for maintaining morale among small business owners dedicated to overcoming the odds. As the director of the Genesis Technology Incubator in Fayetteville, Arkansas explained, "Our experience has been that there is a huge feeling of isolation for many start-up businesses... The incubator keeps them connected to other entrepreneurs in similar situations."[49] In fact, one independent study reported that incubator residents tended to facilitate partnerships with other incubator participants, noting that one out of every six firms reported that they had collaboration with another incubator client.[50] Thus, not only does formal business incubation allow entrepreneurs to escape entrepreneurial isolation by being surrounded by others who are in the struggle just like them, but operating in the same context with other entrepreneurs can also lead to cooperation and collaborations with one another that may not otherwise be developed.

> *Our experience has been that there is a huge feeling of isolation for many start-up businesses… The incubator keeps them connected to other entrepreneurs in similar situations.*
>
> **- DIRECTOR OF GENESIS TECHNOLOGY INCUBATOR, FAYETTEVILLE, ARKANSAS**

Another benefit of incubator synergy is that it provides a team of supporters for entrepreneurs who are enduring the pressures and challenges of building a business, which is not an easy feat at all. Building a business is *really* hard! My position is this: show me an entrepreneur who says that building a business is easy, and I'll show you an entrepreneur who has never built a thriving business. Note that I did not say "started" a business. This is because anyone can start a business, because starting a business is easy. Instead, I used the term "built" a thriving business, and anyone who has ever built a business knows that building a business is hard. All it takes to start a business is coming up with a good business name, registering the business with the state or country in which you live, and setting up an employer identification number with the Internal Revenue Service. When you do these things, you can legitimately say that you have started a business. Some people even take it a few steps further and order some business

The Business Birthing Blueprint

cards with their name on it as "President and CEO," buy a domain name for their business, and put together a website describing the ins and outs of their business. Being able to call themselves a "CEO" or the "President" of the business that they have started brings them a great sense of pride. However, they have only started a business. If you ask them at this point what their experience has been, they might even tell you that starting a business is easy. It's not until they build and establish the business (if they make it this far) that they will be able to tell you the real truth of the matter: *building* a business is really hard!

Many times, the challenges of building a business can drive entrepreneurs to the point of being ready to throw in the towel and go "find a real job." They might become frustrated with the lack of growth, they might grow tired of struggling to identify a customer base to purchase what they are selling, they might get tired of all of the hard work and seemingly little reward, or (and this is a big one) they might grow tired of being broke! Honestly speaking, entrepreneurs are subject to have 99 problems – *really* compelling ones – that can easily drive them to hang up their hat and float their resumes out in the traditional workforce again, hoping for a hit that will rescue them from the start-up struggle. Remaining committed to a fledgling venture that threatens the entrepreneur with failure on a daily basis can be quite difficult! It is for this reason that being surrounded by other entrepreneurs who are sharing the same lived experiences, and who are also trying their best to navigate similar obstacles on the road to entrepreneurial success really helps.

When the disappointments, discouragements and defeats begin to take their toll, all an incubated entrepreneur need do is step away from the desk, walk down the hall, and receive a few words of motivation that encourage them to stay in the struggle. Each of the incubator residents has subscribed to the same belief and is driven by a similar hope: the struggle will eventually pay off and be worth the inevitable success! In my personal entrepreneurial experience, I find it to be true that no one can *really* encourage an entrepreneur like another entrepreneur who is either engaged in or has overcome the challenges of establishing a sustainable enterprise. Well-meaning but naïve, non-entrepreneurial family, friends and associates will do their best to understand and encourage entrepreneurs beyond the self-doubt, mental fatigue, burnout, apprehension and uncertainty about the future that they deal with daily, but as sincere as their efforts are, they usually fall short. However, when other entrepreneurs rally around them to encourage them, something different happens. They are being encouraged and urged on by people who intimately understand what they are feeling and why they are feeling this way without the weary entrepreneur having to say a word. Further, they can give them experience-based words of encouragement and even potential solutions to help them deal with their current season. When they say "It's going to be okay," and "You're going to make it through this," or "If you just keep going, remain persistent, and don't give up, success is inevitable," their words carry much greater weight and credibility than someone who only works a predictable 9 to 5 job and receives a consistent paycheck. Being surrounded by driven, determined entrepreneurial rock stars in a business incubator is a part of what makes the incubator experience a priceless one.

Another benefit of incubator synergy is the culture that organically develops within the context of a business incubator. It is one of mutual assistance and support, which is critical for the growth and development of an entrepreneur and a start-up enterprise. When entrepreneurs have a business question or need help with addressing the myriad of start-up challenges, the answer or solution can often be found among their peers under the incubator's roof. Garrity describes this as a "true entrepreneurial community," as the co-location of so many start-up companies struggling with overcoming the same challenges at the same time, and who also posses a strong commitment to overcome them, creates an opportunity for business owners to share and learn from each other.[51] A culture of helpfulness tends to be prevalent in a business incubator and is characterized by give and take; sometimes entrepreneurs are on the giving end of assistance or information, and other times, entrepreneurs are on the receiving end. Entrepreneurs who have taken up residence in a business incubator are likely to be at different stages of growth and development; those who have been in business longer and have seen success in their early-stage ventures will have more business wisdom and expertise to offer to those who are brand new to the start-up world, and they are typically eager to offer a few words of advice and valuable business insights to their fellow residents.

Those who are brand new to the start-up world also have lots to contribute to the incubator's culture of mutual assistance and support. For example, what they lack in entrepreneurial experience and expertise, new start-up entrepreneurs often make up for in enthusiasm. New start-up developers tend to be full of high hopes and excitement about building "the best business ever," and as a result, they are full of the wide-eyed optimism, energy, enthusiasm and hopefulness that the ups and downs of the entrepreneurial rollercoaster have caused to fade in the lives of many veteran entrepreneurs over the years. Believe it or not, energy and enthusiasm have great value in a business incubator for very good reason: they are key ingredients for creativity! Entrepreneurs in any stage of business growth enjoy having access to other high-energy entrepreneurs who still have an abundance of creative juices flowing and who are eager to contribute their opinions and insights when requested. Creativity can play a key role in helping business owners to develop new ideas, innovating existing products or processes, overcoming obstacles, and inspiring creative approaches to addressing the needs of start-ups. Thus, regardless of how new an entrepreneur is to the world of start-ups, when they reside in a business incubator, they can also contribute to the culture of mutual assistance and support.

Most of all, the culture of mutual assistance and support that develops within an incubator is valuable because it produces an atmosphere in which entrepreneurs pull for one another's success, and rally around one another to ensure that all of the start-ups reach their growth and development goals. Rather than viewing themselves as one individual independent start-up among many others, incubator culture tends to foster a mentality of "we're all in this together" among the incubator residents. This results in the development of a collective identity, one in which entrepreneurs feel connected to their fellow residents and do all they can to contribute to the success of their start-up neighbors. As a result, the start-ups are more likely to collaborate with one another, bounce ideas off of one another, and collectively contribute to the overall success of their fellow incubator residents.

A Multiplicity of Missions:
Categories of Business Incubators

Although the bottom line for business incubators is essentially small business development, differences do exist among incubators, usually in terms of the goals and objectives of the sponsoring organization. Whatever the interest of the sponsoring organization, there is an incubator that will effectively advance their goal of small business incubation. According to the NBIA, incubators reported the following as their mission or goals for incubating businesses, ranked by average rating of importance on a 1 to 5 scale:[52]

- Creating jobs for local community (4.7)
- Fostering community's entrepreneurial climate (4.6)
- Building or accelerating growth of local industry (4.0)
- Diversifying local economies (3.9)
- Retaining businesses in community (3.9)
- Commercializing technologies (3.8)
- Identify potential spin-in/spin-out biz opportunities (3.5)
- Generate net income for incubator/sponsors/investors (3.2)
- Encouraging minority or women entrepreneurship (3.2)
- Generate complementary benefits for sponsoring org (2.7)
- Revitalizing distressed neighborhood (2.7)
- Moving people from welfare to work (2.3)

Incubator experts advise that selecting an industry niche is a good move when developing an incubator, because it allows the incubator to concentrate on the types of equipment, products, resources and services that it invests in for the benefit of its residents. A representative of one incubator organization explains, "If you have a focus—either on a certain type of company or a certain population, like women or minorities—then you're working with people who have the same challenges, who are undergoing the same shared experiences."[53] For example, one incubator that desired to focus on helping minority contractors led the organization to offer courses on such customized topics as blueprint reading and bidding on government contracts.[54]

The InBIA classifies business incubators into five distinct program types:[55]

- Mixed-use incubators (54%)
- Technology incubators (37%)
- Other (5%)
- Manufacturing incubators (3%)
- Service incubators (1%)

Mixed-use Incubators

Mixed-use incubators comprise more than half of all incubators in North America (54%).[56] This type of incubator accepts clients from a wide variety of business emphases. They are largely created by local governments to spur economic growth and create jobs. Mixed-use incubators contain a variety of different types of enterprises including service companies, general contractors, specialty foods vendors, marketing firms, staffing companies, and financial service advisors. Except for restaurant and retail operations, most start-up businesses are well-suited for an incubator.

Technology Incubators

Technology incubators comprise nearly 37% of all incubation programs in North America (a slight decrease from 40% in 2006).[57] These incubators "focus on enhancing community research and development in high-tech, rapid-growth industries that have a good chance of attracting capital and can have a long-term impact on spurring economic growth and creating jobs."[58] While firms in all types of business incubators show similar increases in their annual gross sales, firms from technology incubators create more jobs than other types of incubators.

Manufacturing Incubators

Manufacturing incubators, which comprise approximately 3% of business incubators, provide physical space and technical business assistance for those in the manufacturing industries (usually lighter manufacturing industries). These incubators must often provide ample, large production spaces in order to accommodate the manufacturing needs of their clients.

Service Incubators

Service incubators, which comprise 1% of business incubators, are those which cater their product and physical space offerings to businesses in service industries, including professional services.

Other - Targeted Incubators

Targeted incubators, which comprise fewer than 5% of all incubators, are those that focus on a specific industry such as software, kitchen/food, multimedia, the arts, medical and biosciences, fashion, environment, etc. They may also target populations of a specific demographic like the Houston Women's Business Center for example. This Women's Business Center targets contemporary, fast-track women business owners and career professionals and bills itself as the first incubator to teach entrepreneurship and intrapreneurship to women.[59]

Other - Empowerment Incubators

Empowerment incubators make up the smallest percentage of all incubators and are also sometimes referred to as "microenterprise" or "community" incubators in the literature. These organizations tend to focus on assisting targeted populations in their efforts to develop and grow small business enterprises.

4

So, You Say You Want to Establish an Incubator?

Pertinent Questions to Ponder

Simply by virtue of the fact that you are reading this book, you are either seeking more information about establishing a business incubator, or researching it as a viable option for business development in your community. I dare predict that after reading the chapter on the benefits of business incubation, you are more bought in than ever on the idea of business incubation. I understand your excitement and the passion that is burning within; however it is at this point that we must tap the brakes and help you face your reality by asking some very pertinent questions. Take some time to honestly evaluate the questions presented in this section. You won't regret it in the long-run!

Why Do You Want to Establish
a Business Incubator?

What is your motivation for wanting to start a business incubator? Is it the passion for developing budding entrepreneurs? Is it to develop the community that surrounds you? Is it to provide sources of employment for a depressed community? Is it to be on the cutting edge of the latest industries? Your answer to this foundational question is necessary to define the basic framework for the incubator that you will create. If you are unable to define a clear *why* behind your drive to open a business incubator, *what* you create as an incubator organization will be significantly compromised – especially when things become challenging along the way – and your organization will be unstable.

Among the different factors that stimulate the development of business incubators, the principal motivations underlying the formation of a formal business incubator include: (1) economic development efforts intended to stimulate the economy, create jobs, and diversify the local economic base; (2) the commercialization of research and the transfer of technology into new and different commercial applications; and (3) the enhancement of small business success.[60]

There are a number of different ways that incubators find their origin within a community. For example, the Houston Business Journal featured a story entitled, "New Incubator to Cater to Ex-Enron Employees" in which a group of Houston business people were reported to have launched a nonprofit incubator to help former Enron Corporation employees start new businesses based on their entrepreneurial ideas (the Houston-based company laid off 4,500 people in December 2002 when they filed bankruptcy).[61] At no charge to the entrepreneurs themselves, this organization would offer these newly unemployed individuals secure office space, professional services, computers, mentoring and access to funding sources. The incubation group, Resource Alliance Group of Houston, launched the incubator because according to the co-founder and executive director of the group, there was no way that these people were going to be absorbed into the job market, and "Every (energy) company across the country wants to pick off that talent. We don't want them to leave because of the financial impact on the community."[62] Thus, this particular incubator collaborative was established as a way to keep bright, young talent and their business ideas in the city of Houston.

Another reason that incubators are launched in communities is that community developers or planning boards determine that there is a need for more diversity in the business community. This is especially true when economic and community developers engage in the practice of smokestacking, concentrating large numbers of jobs within a few major corporations or industry sectors. One of the best ways to cushion against the possible shockwaves that a massive layoff or company closing may have on the local economy is through the careful development of stable small businesses. Lawrence Molnar, Associate Director of the University of Michigan Economic Growth Institute and past President of the Michigan Business Incubator Association, explained: "While a variety of development strategies are aimed at attracting existing firms to a region, business incubation is geared primarily to creating new firms and new jobs. In an economy where new businesses are creating far more jobs than existing corporations, it's important for communities to have business creation strategies in place."[63]

Other groups have also become active in the incubator movement for various reasons, including tribal governments, chambers of commerce, church groups, arts organizations, community development councils, federal agencies, colleges and universities.[64] Each of these has a primary motivation in mind when starting their business incubator, from job development to providing an outlet for their students to commercialize the ideas that they invent in the classroom. What's your motivation? Ensure that it is clear.

> *While a variety of development strategies are aimed at attracting existing firms to a region, business incubation is geared primarily to creating new firms and new jobs. In an economy where new businesses are creating far more jobs than existing corporations, it's important for communities to have business creation strategies in place.*
>
> — LARRY MOLNAR, ASSOC. DIR. OF THE UNIVERSITY OF MICHIGAN ECONOMIC GROWTH INSTITUTE

How Will You Finance the Launch of a Business Incubator?

The question of how much of a financial investment one will need when starting an incubator is a very pertinent question to consider in this phase. The start-up costs to launch an incubator vary based on the size and condition of the facility, services offered by the program, and how many residents the incubator will serve. Jumpstarting Business Ventures (JBV) reported that total start-up costs for an incubator can range from $175,000 to over $4 million, with the median being $412,500.[65]

Perhaps the highest financial consideration in opening a business incubator is that of the physical incubator space itself. However, there are creative ways of bringing the idea of an incubator to reality without such a high initial investment. For example, it is not unheard of for a city to sell an unused or abandoned warehouse or office building to a nonprofit organization for $1 (or lease it for $1 a year) as long as the organization agrees to pay for the build-out and maintenance of the facility. However, a word of caution: be careful not to become too overly excited as soon as local governments offer these spaces for incubator use. Before accepting use of the building, make an accurate assessment of whether the renovations necessary to bring the building within compliance of city codes and to properly house incubator residents is within the projected budget of your incubator initiative.

Another option for consideration, if there is no money for a build-out, is to ask the city or even a private corporation, such as a bank, to donate office space in one of their occupied facilities as a starting point for the launch of an incubator. They may donate space on partially-occupied floors, or they may even donate several unoccupied floors of an office building. If you will attempt to go this route, keep your eyes open for news of mergers and acquisitions of large companies and firms on the evening news, because this usually means that all or part of one company will be merged with the other, leaving valuable empty office space unoccupied. You will find that if you are a nonprofit organization doing good things for the community, companies are quite generous in their support of your cause, and while they may not donate money, they will donate operational space if it is available.

The second-highest expense of starting a nonprofit business incubator is usually the staffing. In starting the incubator, while a staff of ten people may be your ideal, in many cases, a staff of two will be your reality: yourself and an administrator. When planning out your facility, plan for the growth of the staff by setting aside office space for future staffers; however, operate according to what your budget can handle so that the staffing issue does not hinder your ability to open the facility. Additionally, since you will be working with limited paid staff, those you do hire will need to be experienced in providing technical assistance in the areas that business owners need, from accounting to marketing, and from technology to capital fundraising. A small staff means that each staff member must wear many hats and fill many roles – all for a salary that may not start out all that hot. Thus, when seeking staff members to work in the incubator, try to locate those with a passion to help others succeed, and appeal to their sense of meaning and significance. People will often accept a smaller paycheck in exchange for the opportunity to do something significant with their lives, whether they define this significance as coming in on the ground floor and helping to build the community's first incubator or as helping the dreams of small business owners come true.

It should also go without saying that in order to compensate for the lack of paid human resources, it will be necessary to tap into various other networks in the community to recruit a good volunteer staff. These volunteers may be solicited as unpaid interns seeking on-the-job resume-building experience from surrounding university or college campuses. Using college students to provide technical assistance to incubator clients is an ideal arrangement for a few reasons: 1) college students are often up-to-date on the latest cutting-edge advancements in various industries and technologies; 2) during their volunteer time working at the incubator, you can screen them over time to determine whether they are ideal candidates for hiring (hiring both undergraduate and graduate college students will cost significantly less than hiring veteran businessmen and women with years of experience); 3) college students are not stuck in their own ways of doing things like established business veterans; instead, they are often fresh, malleable and ready to learn from you about how you desire for them to provide technical assistance and resource support for your incubator clients. In this, simply ensure that there is a good balance of knowledge and training (college students) and on-the-job experience (business veterans) working with your residents in the incubator. If your incubator does not have ready access to a local college or university, or if the campus is not on a public transportation line that can be easily accessed by students, unpaid volunteers may be recruited from small business development organizations or various other business groups that are willing to give a few hours back to the community through helping to develop small businesses.

Public funding is usually solicited to fund incubators. State governments or nonprofit organizations fund roughly half of all business incubators. Most states began including the establishment of incubator programs in their legislation in the 1980's, but over time, due to a slowing economy and a reduced focus on small business development, funding has been cut for programs across the nation, and incubator budgets continue to suffer. Departments of economic development are usually the source of state assistance, but this may vary depending on the nature of the incubator.[66]

In light of this, if public funding will be the primary revenue source for the establishment of your nonprofit business incubator, it may be wise to seek out these sources of funding that are available in your immediate context before launching a plan to build an incubator. In fact, in many cases, people who desire to open business incubators do not attempt to do so until funding is awarded from local or federal government agencies or grant awards have been made from other nonprofit organizations. With this public funding, incubator developers often leverage the funds they have been awarded to solicit private funds from corporate sponsorships to individual donors.

Incubator developers would also benefit from the knowledge that most state-funded incubators focus on technology, and universities and colleges support 27% of the total, making them the second largest incubator sponsors. After this, 8% of incubators are funded by private, for-profit investors, and 16% are jointly funded by public and private sources.[67] Keep these statistics in mind as you establish a design for your business incubator, because if you rely on state funds to finance your incubator, and your particular state tends to lean towards only funding technology-based incubators, you will need to design an incubator with a particularly heavy emphasis on technology.

Although public funding is often used to establish nonprofit business incubators, this is not the only way to launch a business incubator in your community. If you or another organization you know are already a nonprofit organization that is willing to be the sponsoring entity for the incubator, consider making the incubator an outreach of the nonprofit. This may be accomplished through a church that has a business development ministry, a local business development group, a youth organization that desires to nurture youth entrepreneurs or any organization with the space and manpower available to donate to the cause of establishing a business incubator. Having access to the space, paid and volunteer human resources and funding networks of a functioning nonprofit can greatly reduce the amount of capital necessary for the initial launch of a formal incubator program.

Finally, if you find that, despite your passion for business incubation and your drive to develop entrepreneurs, you are unable to finance your dream of opening a brick and mortar incubator facility, consider going virtual with your incubator until you can locate an affordable physical facility. Some of the same support products and services can be offered virtually, and this can actually be a blessing in disguise, as it will allow you to test and tweak your ideas for a while before you implement them as a fixed part of your in-house business incubation program. Testing and tweaking is a necessary step when it comes to developing a formal business incubation program, because not everything will work within every incubator context in exactly the same way!

How Will You Bring the Incubator in Your Mind into Manifestation?

Now that you've read about what an incubator is and the vast variety of benefits that an incubator can offer, I'm sure that your mind has already drifted off at some point to imagine what your incubator will look like, where it will be located, and how many businesses you will help – and you are excited about the opportunity! However, have you asked yourself how you are going to make this happen? If not, this is a critical gap!

Although we will discuss this more in-depth later, I will introduce the notion here: not only will your incubator *house* businesses, you yourself must regard and relate to your incubator *as* a business. This means exercising all of the due diligence that any other start-up business owner would, from developing a feasibility report and business plan to assembling a team to help bring what is on paper into manifestation. Without doing the proper research and legwork up front, your future as an incubator can be as bleak as the outcomes of other entrepreneurs who dive straight in without doing the necessary research and planning: you could go out of business! Do not discount the possibility of this occurring. Lack of due diligence, poor planning and other factors like economic downturns and lack of financial support from stakeholders and sponsors lead to incubation programs closing their doors each year.[68] Therefore, take the time to thoroughly investigate the feasibility of not only starting but sustaining your business incubator before you get started!

Once you work your way through a feasibility plan, you may realize that the incubator you'd envisioned opening up in a few months will actually take more than a year. You might discover that there are not enough financial or human resources in your area to sufficiently serve an incubator, and you need to choose another location. You may find that you lack the relationship networks that are critical for an incubator's success, from financial to business and social connections, and that you need to spend more focused time building your networks. Something that is quite common to find when designing a formal business incubator program is that you might not be able to offer all of the programs and services you desire to offer at the onset due to staffing and potential growth issues. Be diligent to turn over every stone and examine every potential pitfall or challenge to your organization when conducting your feasibility study.

> *Not only will your incubator house businesses, but you yourself must regard and relate to your incubator as a business. This means exercising all of the due diligence that any other start-up business owner would…*

There is no cookie-cutter method for designing an effective incubator, as each incubation strategy will differ with the dynamics of the community that it serves. While research suggests that each incubator is different across genres (whether the nonprofit versus the for-profit genre or the technology/academic/community incubator genres, etc.), it also reveals that there are differences between incubators within the same genres ranging from variations in staff size, facility size, programs offered, admissions criteria, graduation criteria, rent amounts, and services available. For example, some nonprofit incubators serving the community go big, offering a variety of programs and technical services, and other nonprofit incubators are smaller in the scope of what they offer, choosing to provide only critical services on-site and to point their

Small may be the genesis of the 'go big' model

incubator residents towards other partner-organizations in the community that will provide them with the additional assistance they need. While this is a less-than-ideal arrangement (because it has proven to not be as effective as providing the services in-house) it is a viable short-term option until the incubator can offer these support services on-site at the incubator. You decide upon the scope of the services you will offer and the overall design of your incubator program.

If you are going to launch a business incubator, know that the organization will inevitably be a direct reflection of you and your passion for developing start-up businesses; the individual or organization responsible for forming a business incubator greatly affects the makeup and principal focus of the organization. Why? Because the areas of your focus will be evident through the programs, policies, procedures, and levels of accountability and support that you offer to your incubator residents. Such variances in incubator development may take the shape of differences in amount of space dedicated for occupants, services offered, fees charged, entry and spin-out requirements, length of time for occupying incubator space and a number of other factors that differentiate one incubator from another. It's all up to you!

As you develop the design of your incubator, allow me to leave you with this word of advice: whatever you say you are going to offer, whatever you advertise to prospective residents and whatever your website says that you will do for businesses, do it. Doing what you say you are going to do for residents is simply business integrity. As I explained in the introduction, I have not only read about and researched a number of business incubators, but I have traveled around the United States to experience them first-hand. My overall opinion regarding the nonprofit community incubators that I visited was that their operations are insufficient to properly incubate start-up and early-stage businesses. Much to my dismay, most of the incubators seemed to simply be facilities that offer spaces with cheap rent for entrepreneurs. I found most of the organizations, at their cores, to be basic resident-landlord relationships, and this type of relationship is not conducive to the incubation of start-up and early-stage businesses; they require much more hands-on attention and focused interaction to survive and thrive.

During this same research, I also found that overall, most of the literature that the incubators presented to the public through their internet websites and printed marketing materials offered *significantly* more products and services than what was actually being actively offered to and utilized by the incubator clients. Thus, while many of these organizations' models seemed to function ideally on paper, a visit to their incubators, interviews with the managers, staff members and residents, reviews of policy and procedures manuals (or lack thereof) and tours of the facility revealed almost a completely different picture of the inner-workings of the nonprofit incubator. Imagine my dismay, as one who was overwhelmed with excitement about the prospect of business incubation, setting out to visit nonprofit incubator after incubator, only to find that while in concept they were extraordinary, in reality, most of them had a lot of work to do to measure up to their own published standards.

It is for this reason that I caution you to operate with integrity by simply doing what you say you are going to do and offer only those services and resources that you are able to offer – consistently – to your incubator residents. The incubator developers in my research undoubtedly started out just like you: ideal. They saw all of the benefits that an incubator *could* offer and decided to make each of these things a part of their own incubator design. Did they do a feasibility study to determine whether they had access to the resources or to others who could offer the resources before they integrated them into their design? Perhaps. Perhaps not. However, one thing is sure: at one point, they thought they could do it all, but when reality set in – the reality of limited finances, the reality of limited human resources, the reality of how much time and attention each business owner really needed if they were going to survive, and the reality of how much money, time and dedication it would take to keep the incubator afloat – they stopped focusing on their original mission of incubating businesses and switched their focus to keeping the incubator afloat. The "incubator" stayed open, but the mission was aborted... and when the mission of incubation is aborted, the "incubator" is not an incubator at all.

When constructing the design for your incubator, don't be afraid to start small and grow into the support services and resources that you offer. You *can* do everything – you just can't do everything *right now*.

Rome wasn't built in a day. Phase in the resources. Introduce them as manpower as financial resources allow. However, ensure that you can at the *very least* offer the *basics* that are necessary for incubation if you are going to design a business incubator, and if you cannot offer these basic services, now may not be the time for you to establish a formal incubator program. I call the following list the Basic Nonprofit Incubator Starter Program.

Basic Nonprofit Incubator Starter Program

- Reduced-rent office space (size based on program's needs)
- Printer, copier, fax machine, telephone and internet services (in a shared space)
- Conference room or professional meeting space (may be a multi-use or dedicated space)
- Access to funding (from sources with which you have established favor and relationships)
- Access to marketing professionals (from design and delivery to strategy development)
- Access to an accounting professional (either in-house or with a partnering firm at a reduced rate)
- Access to a legal professional (with a partnering firm at a reduced rate)
- Individual mentorship/accountability (at least bi-weekly with incubator manager or local expert)

Take note that each of the professionals featured on the list may be housed on-site at the incubator or outsourced. For example, the marketing professional may double as the accounting professional, or even double as the receptionist, because in a smaller incubator organization, let's face it: there's not much work for the receptionist to do. To be safe, hire for the professional role and then make the receptionist role a part of the job description. The legal professional may double as one of the mentors that provide expert business advice and accountability for the business owner. You may also wear multiple hats, acting as the mentor, the marketing professional and the accounting professional (provided that you are very proficient with a business accounting software like QuickBooks). Whatever you do, plan for yourself and your support staff to be multi-faceted, multi-talented and very busy! However, also keep in mind that it is not ideal for the incubator manager or director to be extremely busy with the in-house workings, because the real work of what the incubator manager does is something altogether different. Keep reading, and you will soon find out why!

When you outsource the skill sets that are not available on-site, ensure that they are outsourced to people with whom you have closely-established relationships. For example, when it comes to saying you offer access to capital networks, this does not mean that you simply know the guy in the loan office at the local bank. It means that you have met with him, discussed your incubator's needs with him, and have developed a formal or at least semi-formal relationship with him to the extent that when you send one of your residents to his office to submit a loan application, he takes the time to review it, discuss where it falls short, and assists the business owner with compensating for any deficiencies that might lead to the loan application's denial. He is not simply "someone you know at the bank," he is an actual partner in the process that is interested in helping you to develop and incubate start-up and early-stage businesses. His interest in seeing the entrepreneur receive funding is as strong as yours, and he will do all that he can do to assist with accomplishing this goal. Then, if the bank says no, he does not simply deliver the bad news to the incubator resident, he provides him with referrals to options B, C and D until sufficient funding comes through.

This same concept holds true with funding resources like venture capitalists and angel investors. Venture capitalists (VC's) are those who look for fast-growing firms into which they can invest money in exchange for a larger-than-average return on their investment into your company, a piece of equity in your company and either a seat on your board of directors or to place one of their people at the top (or nearly at the top) of your company. Angel investors, on the other hand, will often invest money into an organization as a gift or as funding with a minimal return, if any – no huge return on their investment, no placement of their representative in your company, and no equity interest. That has traditionally been the portrait of the angel investor; today, however, we are seeing angel investors (both as individuals and groups) looking more and more like venture capitalists. The point is this: each of these types of funding sources has millions to invest and is looking for the next big thing, and as an incubator manager, you will need to know who they are, where they are, and how to get them to invest in the businesses in your incubator. This is a significant part of your job. Are you ready for it?

Whether they are VC's trying to make big bucks fast or angels that are simply interested in the joy of seeing someone else's business dreams come true (angel investors are often successful entrepreneurs themselves and desire to pay it forward by investing in others' businesses), these investors are literally *looking* for opportunities to plant their funds. In fact, for many years, there has been significantly more funding for good ideas than good ideas to fund. Thus, when you say that your incubator has access to capital networks, just like the relationship you have with the banker, you will need to establish the same type of close relationships with these guys. You've got to find them. You've got to befriend them. You've got to sell them on the idea of your incubator. You've got to get them to buy into the idea of providing funding for the businesses that you have vetted through your incubation process. You've got to "know somebody" in the VC and angel investor world so well that you can pick up the phone, dial them up on their private number, and say, "Hey guy! Have I got an idea for you! Can I bring this new resident over?" This is what I mean when I say you have "access to funding networks."

Just to be clear, access to funding networks does not mean that you can point your incubator residents to a website that has a list of banks that provide SBA (Small Business Administration) loans. It does not mean that you have a brochure entitled "Five Ways to Fund Your Business" that you hand off to your residents that express a need for capital. It does not mean that you were briefly introduced to the local bank president at a luncheon a couple of months ago, and she said "Call me if you need anything," so you send the incubator resident her way to ask for a loan application. No, once you say you provide "access to funding networks" this means that you have a personal, favorable relationship with the people (more than just a few!) that have access to funds and that can tell you where to access some funding for your residents if they are not able to provide funding.

Whether we are discussing access to funding, access to legal professionals, access to accounting professionals, or access to anything else, keep this in mind: access simply means relationship. If you remember nothing else about this section of the book, remember this: the real work of an incubator leader or manager is building relationships – relationships with potential investors, relationships with potential sponsors and donors, relationships with key influencers in the community, relationships with service providers... relationships, relationships, relationships! In building relationships with, say, legal professionals, it is not unusual for the incubator to have two or three standard go-to attorneys that they can send their residents to for pro bono legal advice. These attorneys will donate a certain number of hours each month to help the mission of the incubator, and they will only charge incubator residents – at a reduced rate – for very legal-specific work. Some incubator managers will arrange for business attorneys to come on-site to offer free "ask the legal expert" sessions once or twice a month for the value of incubator clients. These arrangements, again, are simply birthed out of relationship. Businesses inside of a community business incubator will experience benefits of residency only as deep as the levels and networks of relationships developed by the incubator manager.

It is for this reason that I previously mentioned that it is not a good idea to inundate the incubator manager with the day-to-day workings of the incubator. He or she has to be out in the community, shaking hands, gaining favor and building relationships with people that can later be accessed to add value to incubator residents. Incubator managers that are actually incubating businesses should be able to have a resident walk into their office, listen to the client's need for resources or advice, pull up their contact list, pick up the phone and say, "Hey, it's me. Listen, I need a favor. Can I send someone over to you?" You can tell when an incubator manager is not truly incubating businesses: he or she is always in the office, sitting at a desk. Relationships are not built this way. They are built face to face.

In my travels to perform site visits and research at various nonprofit incubators, no one impressed me more than the famous Della

Clark of The Enterprise Center, housed in West Philadelphia in the legendary and beautifully renovated American Bandstand building. The organization she built was, by far, the best example of a highly-effective business incubator as I have ever seen, and she is nationally and internationally known for her unusually high level of effectiveness in successfully incubating each business that is granted entry into the incubator, putting them on a course to soar to phenomenal heights. In fact, this model incubator program has even received the National Business Incubation Association's "Business Incubator of the Year" Award – an amazing feat considering all of the various for-profit and nonprofit incubators in the nation.

At the time that I visited, the already-successful organization was working on how to bring businesses to scale within three years—that is, $3 million in gross revenue within three years of entering the incubator. However, of all that she taught me when I spent time interviewing her and her staff, touring the facility, and learning about her operations, nothing struck me more than the lesson she taught me about her level of effectiveness, and I will never forget it. I asked Clark what she spent most of her time doing as the incubator director. She replied, "Have breakfast with people. Have lunch with people. Have dinner with people. My appointment book stays full." Clark was not in the office much because she was clear on her role: her work was to be the master networker, establishing relationships throughout the community with the major players for the benefit of the businesses she was incubating, and this is a key lesson for any would-be incubator developer to learn. She shared that anyone who is selected to run an effective business incubator program should be a "good traffic cop and a master networker; someone who has a vast network of people; someone who is a great connector."

> I asked Clark what she spent most of her time
> doing as the incubator president. She replied,
> "Have breakfast with people. Have lunch with people. Have
> dinner with people." ... She was clear on her role: to be the
> master networker, establishing relationships throughout the
> community with the major players for the
> benefit of the businesses she was incubating...
>
> - INTERVIEW WITH DELLA CLARK,
> PRESIDENT OF THE ENTERPRISE CENTER

If you are reading through this section and feel that the requirements of an incubator manager or director are not currently descriptive of you (i.e., building relationships and networking are not your strength), you have two choices: learn to become a master networker and connector or hire someone who is. The success of your incubator residents depends on it. If someone has the drive and enthusiasm to learn to network effectively, he or she will be a much more successful incubator manager than someone with an extensive network but a lack of drive to connect incubator clients with individuals in the community. The two must work together, hand in hand.

5

The "Best Practices" Chapter

Important Lessons to Learn before Launching a Business Incubator

By now, you are probably well on your way to constructing your concept of the most effective business incubator there ever was – at least in your head! In order to add some additional depth to your preliminary mental planning, allow me to introduce to you one of my favorite chapters on best practices. You may be wondering why I would describe this as one of my favorite chapters. Right? The answer is easy. This best practices chapter contains advice from the experts. Throughout my research interviews, I tend to always ask the same question to incubator directors, managers and leaders so that others may learn from their experiences. The question is this: What final pieces of advice would you leave for an individual or group planning to launch a formal business incubator in their community? The responses that follow are always golden – the results of years of lessons learned through successes, both carefully planned and serendipitous, and costly failures. An old proverb says that a wise man learns from the successes of others; a fool has to try everything for himself.

It is my hope that you will take advantage of these words of advice that those who are deep in the incubator trenches thought worthy of sharing with other would-be incubator practitioners. While I was not able to use everyone's final nuggets of wisdom, I have carefully featured several of the ones that I consider most pertinent for the beginning incubator developer. Study each one, consider them carefully and learn from them. Doing so will save you time, money and immeasurable frustration as you begin your incubator journey.

Conduct an *Objective* Feasibility Study

As previously discussed, in order to develop an effective incubator, you must approach it as strategically and diligently as a business. Far too many incubator developers place most all of their time and focus into developing the incubator facility. As a result, that's primarily what they end up with – simply a facility that houses businesses (whatever you focus upon, you will manifest!). However, remember, such operations are *not* incubators. An incubator is about providing a program of development to equip, support, connect, and provide resources to businesses that they need to survive and thrive!

Each incubator should be developed just as any business would be, with a strong business plan, with a completed feasibility study, with a financial plan, and with a clear mission and vision. As Lawrence Molnar, Associate Director of the University of Michigan Economic Growth Institute and past President of the Michigan Business Incubator Association, explains: "Creating a business incubation program is the equivalent to creating a new business. It requires capital, investment and effort."[69]

In order to plan your strategy to incubate businesses, it will be necessary to conduct a feasibility study to determine the climate of the community, to assess the community's needs, and to identify a potential market for the incubator. A feasibility study will also help you as an incubator developer to realistically determine the level of support and financial backing that will be required to launch the incubator, and the sources of revenue that will be accessible to sustain incubator operations. If these numbers do not work out on the feasibility study, rest assured, they will not work out in real life. Do not allow your passion to launch lead you where your resources cannot sustain you. In fact, the International Business Innovation Association advises would-be incubator developers to resist the urge to fall in love with a vision for an incubator without first engaging in some sobering considerations. For example, one might ask, *Is there a sufficient market for this incubator?* and *Will I be able to engage the support of businesses, political and civic leaders to partner with me in my efforts?* Taking these things into consideration will help to temper the developer's creativity with a strong dose of reality.

If your carefully-researched feasibility report suggests that your incubator plan is not feasible, don't second guess it – simply accept that it's not feasible. This does not mean that it will *never* be feasible, it just means that for the time being, you need to spend more time planning, getting connected, and setting up access to funding, networks, key influencers, and other resources needed to adequately make your organization run according to its stated mission – not just for today, but for years from now.

If, perchance, your feasibility study screams, "This is NOT feasible!" don't drown out these results with your optimism; listen to them. Do not allow yourself to be in a rush. Consider launching a virtual incubator. Clients will pay a fee to access your support resources online, meet with their mentors at different locations throughout the community and be provided with case-managed services overseen by the incubator director and provided by paid or experienced volunteer staff.

> *Creating a business incubation program is the equivalent to creating a new business. It requires capital, investment and effort.*
>
> **- LAWRENCE MOLNAR, ASSOC. DIR. UNIVERSITY OF MICHIGAN ECONOMIC GROWTH INSTITUTE**

Develop a Team

Research studies suggest that entrepreneurs working in teams of two or more tend to be more successful at sustaining a business enterprise than individuals that go at it alone. I know this to be true first-hand in my own entrepreneurial endeavors: having someone to bounce ideas off of, to share crises and confidential information with, and someone to simply share the load of making a business successful is quite priceless. Yes, it has its challenges and risks, but there is always a greater risk with operating out of the rugged individualist mindset of "I can do it all by myself." Sure, you can do it all by yourself, but it's a whole heck of a lot easier doing it with the right partner.

That being said, remember that your incubator is not just for helping businesses, it *is* a business. There will be loads and loads of work to do – far too much for one person – and having at least one or two people working with you will result in greater effectiveness. You can maintain the lead position of the visionary director/manager that serves as the founder and face of the organization, but your team members should possess your same level of vested interest and buy-in. Such passion and dedication will be necessary to keep your team committed to process when things get rough.

Develop a Strong Network of Relationships

If you've been reading this book carefully, you will have noted, on a number of occasions, my repeated emphasis on the vital importance of developing a strong network of relationships. After all, this is the work of the incubator manager: connecting your incubator residents to investors, experts, key influencers, know-how networks and other resources needed to virtually guarantee the success of the businesses in the incubator. Yes, you will offer to contribute your first-hand expertise to foster their success, but true incubation extends far beyond your own personal contributions. Your ability to effectively incubate your businesses is a direct function of your network of personal, *active*, established relationships with those in the community that can help solve your residents' problems and meet your residents' needs.

To use a very casual colloquialism in our society, this means that you need to be able to "hook up" your business incubator clients in any and every way possible. Need funding? I know somebody that has some money to give, at least enough to get you over this hump. Need a marketing piece designed? I have someone that owes me a favor, and they do great work. Need the inside scoop on what a procurement coordinator is looking for on a particular bid proposal? I played golf with his boss last week, so let me give him a call. Need a hotel in Dallas for a week-long business event? We have a relationship with the local four-star hotel downtown, and I'll let them know we need a reduced rate at their location in Dallas. Need a permit pushed through to make a big sale? I just had lunch with one of the city council members and they'll take care of you. Plainly stated, being able to function in this role is called "having the hook up." "Hook up" is simply a casual term for "connector," and connecting is the real work of the incubator leader... not simply collecting residents' rent!

Never rest on the task of developing your network of relationships! By "developing," I mean the following:

1) Maintain contact with your existing relationships to keep them active, and make efforts to keep yourself and your incubator on their mind; and 2) Work to develop new relationships with people in the community (and beyond) that can help you advance your cause of connecting businesses to others who can help them succeed.

Don't Just Establish a Real Estate Operation!

I cannot emphasize this point enough. While a number of nonprofit and community business incubators promote themselves as true business incubators in their literature and on their websites, their reality of actually incubating businesses falls short of their stated mission. They are not incubators at all; they are merely real estate operations that house a number of entrepreneurs under one roof with a few shared resources and perhaps a how-to business seminar offered every now and again.

Again, I am confident that when they started out, they held the same passionate aspirations as you and I, but over time, as a result of having to make the rent and keep the incubator facility running, their focus shifted towards such. Sure, they would put up flyers about an upcoming seminar that a volunteer was offering on taxes, advertisement, or something else that *should* be of interest to the start-up and early-stage entrepreneur, but these efforts could scarcely be called incubation. Couple that with the fact that few, if any, of the entrepreneurs would attend these seminars because there was no accountability for their continuous learning process, and it all boils down to a mere real estate operation.

Whatever you do, always maintain as your primary focus the incubation of the business. As a result of your success in doing so, when you seek funding, the resources will follow. Let your works and successes speak for you in your funding pitches. Especially when seeking public funding for incubator operations, successful statistics are hard to question. Are your incubator clients increasing the amount of tax dollars in the community through business development? Are your clients creating jobs and putting people to work? Are your clients engaging in the socially responsible behavior of giving back to the community? Funding follows such success stories, because these are the types of programs that local and state governments, corporate sponsors, foundations and private donors desire to sustain.

Seek Funding Early

Like a business, an incubator requires an adequate amount of capital for its start-up and sustainability. It takes more than a few pennies to launch and maintain an effective business incubation program! For example, Jumpstarting Business Ventures reported that total start-up costs for an incubator can range from $175,000 to over $4 million, with the median being $412,500.[70] Then, the InBIA reports that the average annual incubation program revenue was approximately $540,000 in 2012, and the average incubation program expenses were approximately $517,000 for the same year (both lower amounts than reported in 2006). This should emphasize the importance of funding in establishing and maintaining your incubator.[71]

These are not small budgets that you might haphazardly stumble upon and manage to pull together. You will need a *really* strategic funding plan! Although there are ways to cut costs as we have previously discussed, incubator developers should have a funding strategy that answers the funding questions: 1) how much funding have we received? 2) what sources of funding do we expect to receive and how frequently? 3) how will we coordinate fundraising efforts? 4) where will we go to request funding? and (this is my favorite, ever-significant, most critical question!) 5) whose job is it going to be to pursue these funds for us?

Because it is unlikely that 100% of an incubator's funding will come from one source, in order to be effective in funding the development of a business incubator, developers must become masterful at piecing together a budget comprised of funds generated from a variety of sources. It is only in approaching funding in this manner that an incubator can hope to be sustaining in the long-term. Further, the more sources that you successfully engage and can persuade to commit to your cause, the greater likelihood that you will be able to attract additional supporters and funders to support your cause.[72] Most times, incubator developers are able to find a primary funder in an economic development organization or through a city, county or state government agency. According to the NBIA, in 2012, 25 percent of incubators in North America had primary sponsors that were economic development organizations, although this number was down from 31 percent, which was reported in 2006. Additionally, 16 percent of incubation programs reported being sponsored by city, county and state governments, although this number also fell from 21 percent, which was reported in 2006.[73]

Be advised that your ability to secure funding will be influenced by the economic climate. If the economy is prospering, public and private sponsors will be more likely to release the funds you need to further your mission, but during times of economic downturn, expect for them to tighten their grip on their pocketbooks. However, there is good news, according to the NBIA: despite incubators experiencing a decrease in their revenues over the past several years, many incubators report that they have still been able to maintain a solid financial position. In fact, only 18 percent of incubators in North America who reported receiving a cash operating subsidy (funds provided from a major funding source) reported that if they lost this subsidy, they would have to close their doors. Then again, one-third of incubators do not receive a cash operating subsidy at all.[74] All of this is to say that it can be done: you can develop a sustainable budget that will keep your incubator in business despite the fluctuations in the economy... but you must have a funding plan and a person or persons committed to working the funding plan!

My favorite question in the funding discussion is always the "who" question, because incubator developers may grow restless and anxious during the money discussion. They come up with how much they need, where they will request funding, and what will be done with the funds during their group strategy sessions, but it never fails that they miss the all-important "who" question. By observation, I've even noticed how the "who" question is often missed. The conversation usually sounds like this: "We will approach this corporation and that corporation, and then we are going to apply for at least one grant per month, which should be fairly reasonable without being overwhelming, and then we will go to the university library where I hear they have books listing the thousands of organizations who contribute to entrepreneur programs... it's all very feasible." The question that flies under the radar is and goes unasked is, "Very feasible for *whom*?"

Whenever planning involves the use of "we" instead of "you" or "I," little will ever get done. When it comes down to it, w*ho* is going to do the tedious work of researching and writing the grants? *Who* is going to put together the sponsorship proposals? *Who* is going to make visits to the funding agencies throughout the city? *Who* is going to research the thousands of foundations out there that provide funding for community initiatives? Getting these things done is way more than a notion – that's why few individuals want to do them... and that's why they often go undone. It takes hard work, lots and lots of time, focus and resilience, because in your quest for funding, if you are doing it right, you will hear "no" a lot. However, it often only takes getting a "yes" from a few of the right funding sources to sustain the operations another year, and hearing these "yes's" are worth all of the "no's" in the world. The one who seeks the funding has to be a special person. Just make sure you know "who" this will be before you begin an incubator launch.

Use an Advisory Board to Screen and Counsel Prospective Start-Up Clients

This tip goes along with the tip to develop a team, but since it is so important, it deserves a mention of its own. Whom you select for residency in the business incubator is as important as the incubator operations themselves. These businesses must be able to demonstrate a clear potential for growth and expansion with the help of incubation, so making the right selections is critical. The more limitations on space you have in the incubator facility, the more critical these selections will become. After all, if you have space for 20 businesses, you can afford a couple of false starts (hopefully you will not have any, but things do happen!); however, if you only have room as a start-up incubator for six businesses, for example, you do not have any room for error. Every business granted entry into the small incubator must be as close to a sure thing as can be predicted, and there is no room to gamble. Everything from the entrepreneur's business idea, to the business plan, to the his or her experience, character and resume need to be considered. An incubator's success is largely dependent upon comprehensively screening and admitting the right kind of start-up businesses. Considering that there are so many critical decisions to be made, and with so much on the line for your incubator organization, why would you want to make these decisions alone?

I am sure that you have impeccable judgment, but many expert minds are better than one, and there is safety in a multitude of counsel. Rather than solely relying on the character and business assessment skills of the incubator manager, experts recommend that you put together a committee that is represented by each of the following industries to screen potential incubator residents: legal, banking, capital-raising, small business advising, and marketing. Include as many heavy-hitters as you can, and always try to include a well-known investor in the community.

If possible, once you put this advisory board together, you should also consider using the same board to counsel start-ups. Even if they cannot send their own monies, skills or expert resources your way, they often know someone who can. Even as incubators are faced with providing more services with less money, advisory boards can fill in some of the gaps that a staffing shortage may produce.

Don't Seek Small Businesses, Seek Embryonic BIG Businesses!

Speaking of screening businesses for residence in the incubator, this morsel of advice also demands to stand alone to command the attention that it deserves. This strategy was inspired by the former President and CEO of the Technology Enterprise Center in Jacksonville, Florida (which, unfortunately, is no longer in operation), Al Rossiter, who offered an important perspective of the client companies it sought to attract and incubate: "What we're looking for are companies that can grow to a very significant size... We're not looking for small businesses. We're looking for embryonic big businesses."[75]

> *What we're looking for are companies that can grow to a very significant size... We're not looking for small businesses. We're looking for embryonic big businesses.*
>
> – AL ROSSITER, FORMER PRESIDENT AND CEO OF THE TECHNOLOGY CENTER, JACKSONVILLE, FL

Susan Matlock, President and CEO of Innovation Depot (developed in 2007 as a result of a merger between the Entrepreneurial Center, an incubator that she founded 10 years prior, and which she led at the time of the interview, and the Office for the Advancement of Developing Industries, a high-tech incubator formerly at the University of Alabama Birmingham) maintained a similar position, explaining, "On the front end, we don't just lease space... what I'm looking for are companies with growth potential. I am not trying to serve the self-employed individual, and there's nothing wrong with that; it's just not what I'm doing."

Matlock was saying that self-employed individuals do not make for high-growth companies. Consider this: a family medical doctor with her own private practice is a self-employed individual. Does she have high growth potential, or the capability to grow a large company around the medical services she offers, or is her growth potential limited? An insurance agent is a self-employed individual and may have a few people working for him. Does he have high growth potential, or the ability to grow the company to such a size that it can employ hundreds of people or even scores of workers? A professional master sculptor is self-employed. Does he have high growth potential, or the ability to create a large enterprise around what he does? Each of these may grow their revenue as their clientele expands, but their growth potential is limited because they are *self*-employed. The self-employed are often not ideal candidates for business incubation, because no matter how much they grow, they are severely limited in their ability to become a big business. Embryonic big businesses are small businesses that have the capacity to grow into big businesses in big facilities with big staffs that generate big revenue. Thus, if a small business does not clearly have the capacity to expand into a big business, it is not a fit for business incubation. Regardless of how much space you have to fill in your incubator, do not compromise on this! With practice, over time, you will develop the intuition to discern embryonic big businesses from small businesses that may be limited in their growth potential.

Staff for Growth

When staffing your incubator, the general idea is to hire only the staff you need and can afford at the present time. For example, while your ideal incubator staff might be comprised of eight people operating in key positions, your reality, which is shaped by your budget rather than your desires, might be that you can only afford two people for now: yourself as the incubator manager and someone else who will wear many hats. Being constrained by such limitations, one skill that this other staff person should necessarily have is the ability to provide technical assistance to incubator clients.

Regardless of what type of business incubator you establish, there will also be a great need for technical assistance staff, as these individuals are critical to the incubation process. Technical assistance is simply a fancy-pants term that refers to help that is provided according to the needs of the entrepreneurs, needs which will vary from start-up to start-up. Incubator clients can request marketing technical assistance, tax technical assistance, accounting technical assistance, or assistance in any number of areas where they have need. Since so much of what is required by incubator residents is technical assistance, consider two things when staffing this area: 1) hiring two part-time people who can provide, for example two specialized technical skills each (their skills distinctly differ from one another) instead of one full-time person offering two specialized skills; and 2) bringing in your part-time technical assistance providers in the evenings instead of the daytime.

Think about it: during the daytime, your business owners are working their businesses, making sales, delivering products and services, and marketing to their clients. The evening is when all of the activity and busyness of the day usually dies down, a time when they can sit down with the technical assistance providers to ask critical questions and receive the expert advice they need. Appointments can be set with these technical assistance providers, or these advisors may meet with several residents at once who are facing the same issues. Perhaps you will only need to pay these part-time technical assistance providers to come in every other week, if this is what your incubator clients demand. This will save you money and will save your technical assistance providers from feeling like their services are not needed. Staff only for what your clients demand, when they demand it, rather than for what the textbooks suggest as the ideal incubator staff, and then, as resources allow, grow your staff's presence accordingly.

Don't Reinvent the Wheel

Undoubtedly, you have heard this before, but success is not about what you know, it's about what you practice – and many of us reinvent the wheel all of the time. Therefore, let me remind you that if someone else in the community is offering the same resource that is readily and easily available for access by your resident entrepreneurs, use what they offer. For example, if there is a sales tax seminar that is already in existence, shown to be beneficial and available for your use, why develop your own training or seminar for incubator clients? Bring the organization that does the sales tax seminar into the incubator and let them do it for you!

Here's another example: if you need to develop a form for reserving the conference room or a checklist for the incubator open house, do a search on the internet first for these resources instead of spending hours on them, starting from scratch to develop them yourself! Once you find something similar to what you need, adapt the form or use it as a template – this will save you hours, especially when you find the resources of other business incubators online (don't be afraid to include the key words "business incubator" in your search). The same can be said for other seminars, teaching, training, curriculum development, form development, or anything else that you may have to spend time generating. Before you generate anything from scratch, always ask, "Is it possible that someone has done this already?" and then begin your search with the internet. You will soon discover that the World Wide Web is a splendid, time-saving tool, especially for the life of a business incubator manager. You'll be amazed at what other business incubator leaders have put out there.

Join the InBIA (The International Business Innovation Association)

I paid homage to this organization in the Introduction, and I must do so again, because yes, it's just that important. Incubators that are members of the InBIA served twice as many client companies and produced nearly twice as many graduates as non-member incubators did, on average. Further, incubators with membership in the InBIA had client companies that created one-third more jobs than client companies from nonmember incubators on average.[76] You don't know what you don't know until someone tells you what you don't know. One thing you will find out when you join the InBIA is that, despite reading this book, there is a lot that you don't know. As an expert researcher on incubators, I do know a lot, but there's still a lot that I don't know! I would encourage you to join the InBIA as soon as you determine that the incubator route is the way you want to go.

6

The Business behind the
Brick & Mortar

The Operations of a Formal Business Incubator

Up to this point, we have provided an overview of what one might
expect when entering a business incubator. By now, you should have a
general idea of what an incubator is, what an incubator does, what the
work of an incubator manager is, and various considerations that
should be taken into account when building a business incubator. Now,
we will move further away from theory and toward a practical
discussion of each of the aspects of operation within a business
incubator. This will prepare prospective business incubator developers
to establish these enterprise centers. The discussion will be broken into
three phases: entry operations, entrepreneurial development
operations and exit operations.

Table 2. Three Phases of Business Incubator Operations

PHASE 1:	PHASE 2:	PHASE 3:
Entry Operations	Entrepreneurial Development Operations	Exit Operations
1. Business plan	1. Incubator Manager	1. Graduation and spinning out
2. Application criteria	2. Accountability process	2. Exit interview
3. Application process	3. Residency requirements	3. Incubator alumni
4. Screening criteria	4. Mentoring	
5. Interview with Board of Advisors	5. Funding	
	6. Technical assistance	
6. Awarding of residency	7. Value-added benefits	
7. Orientation	8. Social entrepreneurship	
	9. Facility procedures	

Phase 1: Entry Operations

Business Plan

There are usually a few standard-for-the-industry criteria for admission of potential residents into a business incubator. First and foremost, a business is evaluated on a completed business plan, which should "show a clear demonstration of a market, meaning there are people who are ready, willing and able to buy the product or service."[77] If the business plan is sound but in need of some refining, a business may be admitted entry (after the application and interview process), and the incubator staff will assist with further development of the plan.

Application Criteria

Prior to encouraging businesses to engage in the application process, the business must meet certain basic criteria. If one or more of these criteria are not met, the business should not pursue the application process at the incubator. Please note that basic criteria will differ from incubator to incubator and that the following are only sample criteria:

- Must be at least 18 years of age
- Must be able to prove residency in the county
- Must have been in business more than 6 months but less than 24 months
- Must not be a catering business (unless you have built in a catering kitchen)
- Must not have been convicted of a federal offense
- Must be able to provide at least three years of recent tax returns

Application Process

Each incubator, regardless of type, must have a standard application process. Note when we use the word "process," we are referring to more than simply having an application itself. The application process should clearly spell out the following process in the incubator's print and online literature, and it should be provided somewhere on the application itself:

1) How to obtain an application
2) How the completed application should be submitted back to the incubator for review
3) How long it will take for the applicant to hear back about the status of the application
4) What the review process for applications is
5) Whether or not there is an application fee, and if so, how the fee should be submitted

Prior to developing a new application from scratch, we advise searching the internet for several versions of incubator applications and adapting the one that best fits your application requirements. Ensure that your board of advisors or screening board members review the application to ensure that it is thorough prior to publishing it to the general public.

Screening Criteria

When applications are received from potential business incubator residents, they should be screened by the board of advisors to determine their fit with the basic criteria. Incubator managers and advisory board members must use keen business intuition to evaluate intangibles such as the character, the passion, the commitment and the drive of the entrepreneur. The business owner should show a desire for guidance and direction from the incubator staff in business and technical matters and must demonstrate an openness and willingness to learn from the expertise of incubator managers.

The business must also fit within the scope of the incubator's industry niche, whether it is technology, light industrial or manufacturing, empowerment, or any other industry subgroup (arts, media, service, food production, wholesale distribution) to which tenancy may be restricted. Screeners should take factors into consideration such as how many businesses the incubator currently hosts in any particular industry sector, the uniqueness of the business idea, and how the business can serve the needs of the incubator itself or its residents. For example, if the potential resident business offers computer technical assistance, website development, painting, construction, security systems, etc., these would be of value to the incubator because the company could potentially provide in-house services to other incubator residents, likely at a discount negotiated by the incubator manager in exchange for a reduced rental rate. Considered to be permanent residents, such businesses are often sought after because they have key specialties, like commercial or professional services, that could be of great value to other incubator clients.

The following standard screening criteria should be considered for each potential applicant, although it should by no means be considered an exhaustive, one-size-fits-all list:

- **Type of business**

  Is it a good fit along with other businesses in the incubator? Do we have too many of this type of business already? If so, consider passing for the sake of diversification.

- **Capacity of the business to grow**

  Is the entrepreneur self-employed? Does the business have the unlimited potential to expand? Is this a small business, or is it an embryonic big business in the making?

- **Number of years in business**

  How long has the business been in operation? If longer than a few years, why hasn't the business grown? What are the potential underlying reasons for the business' lack of growth – too much competition in the industry? The instability of the business owner? If the business has been in business less than 6 months, it may be necessary (though not always!) to hold off on making a decision until the applicant has proven his ability to grow and expand.

- **Employment status of the entrepreneur**

  My advice is to carefully consider whether or not you will incubate two-career entrepreneurs – those who only work their small business on the side. These types of entrepreneurs have divided loyalties and are unable to focus solely on the success of the business; and yet this type of focus and dedication is what is needed in an incubator setting. A business owner should commit to working his business full time in order to be allowed residency in an incubator.

- **Marital status, family structure and employment status of spouse**

While this particular criterion may seem a bit nitpicky, I have valid reasons and strong beliefs behind submitting it as part of the screening criteria. Here is why: if entrepreneurs are married and they are the sole providers for their families, when things get rough financially, they may be forced to abandon the start-up business for the present time and get a job that pays a consistent salary to take care of their spouse and children. Once they take on this second job, their business becomes secondary, and they are no longer in the position to be incubated, for they are unable to carry out the instructions and plans laid out for them by their mentors and incubation experts. Eventually, these business owners, who we will rarely see after they take on a second job, end up merely taking up space in the incubator that could be used for another business desperate for incubation. Screening criteria should beware of any characteristic of the entrepreneur that could potentially compromise his ability to fulfill his commitment to a long-term relationship with the incubator.

- **Size of business, growth rate and space needs**

When you are screening potential incubator residents and you only have room for a couple of businesses that can accommodate about four people each in the available space, you cannot very well grant residency to a business that currently needs room for three, but within the next six months, at the rate it is growing, will need room for seven. Take into account the business' growth rate so that you do not set it up for failure by placing it in a space that is projected to be too small in the near future. Instead, if the business is considered a good fit, put it on the incubator's waiting list.

- **Education and experience**

All things being equal, if a decision has to be made between granting residency to a business owner who has corporate or professional business experience versus one who does not, it is often a good idea to go with the one with corporate experience. Why? Because when it comes to learning about navigating the business world, marketing, accounting, and other professional skills, his learning curve will be smaller than someone who is learning these skills from scratch. The same holds true for educational level: all things being equal, it is a better idea to go with the candidate with the greater education (and yes, I am aware that as a rule of thumb, as education increases, entrepreneurial drive increases; however, keep in mind that this is a comparison of entrepreneurs with all things being equal). This can be a touchy subject, but remember that your incubator is a business, and you are not in the business of sparing feelings; you are in the business of growing businesses using the best, most qualified candidates available. Higher professionalism, greater industry experience and higher education simply make a candidate more qualified.

- **Ability to secure financing**

How the business will be financed is an essential deciding factor of whether the entrepreneur will be granted admission into the incubator. If the business has already secured financing from an investor, if it does not require much capital to start up, if it demonstrates that it can be financed by the usual bootstrapping methods (credit card debt, savings, or family and friends), or if it is strong enough to secure traditional financing from banks or other lending institutions, its chances will increase for becoming an incubator resident.

- **Support networks and connectedness to community**

Assessing an entrepreneur's ability to access support networks is a pretty big deal. Being a business owner can be a stressful life, especially considering that in its infancy, there are long work hours, little pay and little reward. Too often, entrepreneurs (especially brand new ones) may become discouraged and decide to close the business down if they do not have support networks that provide encouragement and resources for them. This support may come in the form of providing childcare if the entrepreneur is a parent, especially if a child is sick or needs to be picked up from school in the middle of the day. This support may come in the form of providing emergency funding if the entrepreneur needs gas for his car or a loan to pay his electricity during a particularly lean financial time. It may come in the form of borrowing a couple of friends' trucks to make an especially large delivery. Perhaps most importantly, this support may come in the form of cheering him on, providing an extra set of hands on a project, championing his business throughout the community and providing a listening ear and word of encouragement during a particularly rough day. The entrepreneur's access to support networks is also related to his connectedness to the community, because if he is an isolationist that has very little contact with anyone (family, friends, church members, social organizations, etc.), he is less likely to have the support that is necessary to actively encourage him along the way and help sustain him during his entrepreneurial journey. Thus, take into consideration, the entrepreneur's access to support networks, because his success in the incubator will be tied directly to it.

- **Contracts and business deals pending**

Sometimes, small businesses are thrust into a position in which they are forced to grow at a rapid rate to meet a client's demands or risk failure. This is not an unusual occurrence for small business. Many times, they will submit their names for local city or state government contracts – big ones – or they may submit their companies' names as candidates to place thousands or even hundreds of thousands of their products into a large chain store. Then, much to their surprise, they are awarded the contracts and must find a way to produce for their new clients. Often, they have neither the infrastructure, nor the manpower, nor the funds available to order the inventory necessary to fulfill their clients' needs, and they are looking for some fast help so that their businesses can use these deals to launch them to the next business level. If this is the case with an incubator applicant, screeners need to know. Perhaps these big contracts are just the start of a national expansion of products and services, and the help they will receive in the business incubator will be the key!

- **Past entrepreneurial ventures**

  There are such people as serial entrepreneurs: entrepreneurs who tend to establish enterprise after enterprise, often for the challenge or the thrill of conquering an entrepreneurial goal. Screeners should know if they are dealing with a newbie entrepreneur, a serial entrepreneur, or someone in-between. If a person has had past entrepreneurial success and either sold the company, was acquired by another company, or merged it with another company in which he still has equity, screeners should be aware of this. There is something to be said for those who are unafraid to venture out and start a business; their fearlessness, their drive and aggression and their knowledge of the entrepreneurial process make them an ideal commodity for a place like an incubator. With the proper incubation and support systems, there may be no limit to what they can accomplish!

Interview with a Board of Advisors

Every incubator applicant that passes the first round of screening should be granted an in-person interview with the incubator manager and the board of advisors. This may occur in one or two phases: 1) the incubator manager may opt do the preliminary interview, and if it seems like the candidate is a good fit, invite him or her to interview with the board; or 2) the incubator manager and the board of advisors may all interview the prospective resident at the same time. The questions asked during the interview process should aim to answer the following:

1) Does the candidate meet all of the appropriate screening criteria?
2) Does the candidate's business idea have the potential for exponential growth?
3) Does the candidate appear passionate about the business idea *and* its potential?
4) Does the candidate appear to be open to being mentored and incubated (or is he simply looking for cheap rent)?
5) Does the candidate have any experience or education in business at any level?
6) Does the candidate appear to be a clear, well thought-out and organized thinker?
7) Does the candidate communicate and express his thoughts clearly?
8) Does the candidate appear to be professional or at least semi-professional?
9) Does the candidate appear to be a person of integrity and character?
10) Does the candidate's personality appear to be a good fit with the other incubator residents?

Advisory board interviews with prospective incubator residents should be scheduled on one standing calendar day each month, unless special meetings are called. Remember, the members of your board of advisors should be high-powered community influencers, and these individuals are often very busy, so it is important to make the most efficient use of their time (it is for this reason the option is provided to pre-screen and 'weed out' those who will clearly not be a good fit for the incubator before bringing candidates to the table with the board members). Interviews with each candidate should take no more than 20 – 30 minutes each. If necessary, an additional round of interviews, perhaps with subcommittees of the board of advisors, may be scheduled to ask additional questions of candidates and get a greater feel for their fit within the incubator.

Further, each board member will note their impressions of the candidates on a standard interview scoring sheet (before developing one, search the internet!), and these sheets should be kept in the candidate's application file for future reference. At the conclusions of the interviews, board members will discuss their impressions and vote on granting residency to the candidates that have been interviewed. Please note that it is not a requirement to grant admission to anyone who has been interviewed, and board members should not feel obligated to make a decision about allowing entry to businesses that are not a perfect fit simply to fill empty incubator space.

Awarding of Residency

Notices about being granted space in the business incubator should be made via a formal letter presented on incubator letterhead. The congratulatory award letter should specify the following:

1) Notice of awarding of space in the incubator
2) The amount of space awarded in the incubator (square footage, number of offices)*
3) The amount of rent that the resident will pay and when the first payment is due
4) The term of the lease in the incubator
5) The first date available for move-in into the incubator
6) The new resident's orientation date
7) A formal request to accept or decline the space in the incubator by a certain date

*When the incubator is first launched, tours of the facility may occur on the day of the interview. After the initial set of residents is established and the incubator has been functioning, the potential resident should have the opportunity to tour the available space prior to the interview process.

Orientation

Each incubator resident should be required to participate in an orientation that provides details about the expectations, policies and procedures of residency in the incubator. Ideally, this orientation would be led by the incubator manager, but it could also be led by a capable assistant with knowledge of the ins and outs of incubator residency. Ensure that the orientation is as professional and thorough as possible, as this will be the resident's first introduction to the inner workings of the organization, and as incubator staff members are the models for how residents relate to the program, it is necessary to set a high standard. It is also a good idea to have at least one other incubator resident present at the new resident's orientation to answer any questions he might have from a resident's perspective. The orientation presentation should include but not be limited to:

1) What to expect in the business incubator
2) Incubator hours of operation (and after-hours policies) and access procedures
3) Incubator security procedures
4) Shared office equipment policies and procedures (any copy codes or long distance codes to equipment should be disseminated at orientation)
5) Incubator resident expectations (meetings, continuing education, monthly meetings, etc.)
6) Where to go to receive various services offered by the incubator
7) Office cleanliness and upkeep of common areas
8) Maintenance request procedures
9) Incubator visitor policy (signing incubator guests in and out)
10) Parking policies
11) Incubator's policy concerning pets in the office
12) Graduation or spinning out policy

Phase 2: Entrepreneurial Development Operations

Incubator Director or Manager

The incubator director or manager role is the most critical in the business incubator and deserves some in-depth attention in a discussion of incubator operations. These key individuals link incubator residents to the outside world, and they are often referred to as "influencers" or "executive champions" who make things happen and who are able to network with other influencers to make the right connections for the benefit of the businesses in the incubator.[78] These highly-networked, important, influential individuals provide the vision and inspiration necessary for nurturing and maintaining the incubator environment. In fact, the incubator manager, described as the "impresario" or the "great man," has been found to be the most important intervention tool for incubator resident success.[79] Greene and Butler note that "this role, like every other aspect of incubators, varies widely between incubators, but includes a selection of responsibilities such as networking, counseling, providing emotional support, and providing expertise in diverse areas as marketing, business operations, finance, and accounting."[80] These incubator influencers also link together the research university, large technology companies, small technology companies, state government, federal government, community leaders, people to know, and support groups.

> *[Being an incubator director] includes a selection of responsibilities such as networking, counseling, providing emotional support, and providing expertise in diverse areas as marketing, business operations, finance, and accounting.*
>
> **- DR. PATRICIA GREENE AND DR. JOHN SIBLEY BUTLER ON THE CRITICAL ROLE OF INCUBATOR MANAGEMENT**

I cannot emphasize enough that incubator managers must be more than merely landlords. Rather, they must be intelligent, network-savvy, and masterful at forging alliances with those in the community, including professionals who can donate their services as mentors and investors and they must be resources in and of themselves, able to provide technical assistance in a number of areas to entrepreneurs (the great majority of all senior incubator managers have a college degree or post-graduate education). A Rutgers University study examining incubators as a part of the strategic framework for commercial revitalization noted a critical role that these managers play: "Incubators may forge partnerships with lending institutions and potential investors. They may also create co-provider, co-bidding, joint selling or distribution arrangements for their firms. It would be difficult, if not impossible, for an individual firm to create such a vast network of services and resources on its own."[81]

For example, incubator management might be approached by a resident who is experiencing a legal dispute with a distributor and may not possess the resources or the know-how to address the settlement of the dispute. After a visit to the incubator manager, the owner is contacted by an attorney in the community who offers his services to the resident free of charge to assist in settling the dispute. Such relationships are often almost single-handedly based on the incubator manager's networks in the community with professionals willing to donate their time to the cause of the incubator and its residents. Ultimately, the role of the business incubator is to create a safe place, a microcosm of the best possible entrepreneurial community that can provide a synergy among business, academic, government, and community entities.

Accountability Process

A large part of the true process of business incubation is maintaining close accountability with incubator residents in order to ensure that they are following the growth and development plan that they co-created with the assistance of the incubator manager and their mentoring team. These plans include goals and objectives, benchmarks and action plans designed to be carried out by the entrepreneur.

However, it is easy for an entrepreneur to become distracted by the day-to-day details of working a business and not focus on specific tasks designed for their overall development. Anything that is not consistently evaluated cannot be expected to produce desired results; thus, the entrepreneur's progress should be monitored through regularly scheduled, preferably monthly accountability sessions. During these sessions, the business owner will have an opportunity to share his or her progress, request any assistance needed, and receive expert advice and encouragement from the incubator leader.

Some experts also recommend close accountability regarding incubator residents' financials, although perhaps not so frequently as on a monthly basis. During financial accountability sessions, business owners should provide accurate financials that present a comparative view of income and expenses, and they should also provide financial projections at least six months ahead. Residents are asked to provide these financial statements to incubator managers so that the management stays ahead of the business's growth trends and development.

Residency Requirements

Residency requirements simply refer to the formal guidelines to which companies must adhere once inside an incubator. They vary according to incubator organization, with some programs being more structured and rigorous while others are less formal and more laissez-faire. Any meetings, trainings, codes of conduct or other behaviors that are required as stipulations of incubator residency should be clearly specified in writing for incubator residents upon their move-in to the facility.

One of the primary requirements that tends to be standard among business incubators is the requirement that companies purchase proper insurance coverage for the business, usually not less than $1 million as a condition of maintaining residence in the incubator. Requirements may also entail such activities as attending a minimum number of one-hour business development sessions per month, keeping regularly-scheduled meetings with the mentoring team, showing courtesy to other incubator guests by not entering their spaces or utilizing their possessions without permission, or even the requirement to keep noise levels at a minimum and to keep all business dealings confined to their assigned incubator spaces. The residency requirements will differ by type of incubator and will be determined by the incubator manager. Prior to reinventing the wheel, however, we recommend searching online for existing incubator residency requirements and adapting them for your own incubator's use.

Mentoring

A large part of incubating a business is providing incubator clients with access to powerful and well-networked key influencers in the community that can provide expert advice, access to capital resources, access to know-how networks and that will leverage their influence and relationships to help the incubator business thrive.

As a best practice, each incubator business should have its own mentoring team (though one team may serve more than one incubator resident if the businesses are similar in nature). The mentoring team should not be homogeneous; it should be hand-picked by the incubator manager according to the needs of the entrepreneur, featuring an expert in the entrepreneur's industry, a financial representative, a legal representative, a marketing representative, and a business development expert – much like the composition of the board of advisors. Each incubator resident is required to attend regularly-scheduled meetings with his mentoring team and is strongly discouraged from canceling at any time.

Funding

Because connecting businesses to funding is perhaps the most important resource that incubators can offer their residents, it should be one of the most critical topics when discussing incubator operations. Incubators are about bringing together a variety of financial resources on the local, state and national levels, through both public and private funds, to be able to provide financial assistance to entrepreneurs who desperately require these infusions of capital in order to survive and prosper. These incubator monies often come in the form of public and private grants, endowments, research awards, special government programs, and through the donation of private funds. The use of these funds is typically restricted to financing the purchase of inventory, supplies, raw materials, equipment, machinery, and working capital and often are not authorized for the entrepreneur to pay existing debt, to purchase real estate or to make business investments.

Incubators may provide access to funding in one of two ways. The first means of providing funding is for the incubator to build an in-house resource pool to which qualifying incubator residents have access. These funds are typically offered as low-to-no interest microloans ($100 to $25,000) that do not follow traditional lending criteria, placing less emphasis on credit reports, assets and collateral, than do traditional lending institutions. Incubator program participants may apply for microloans to finance the operational needs of their business. Also, if the incubator offers such a service, they may apply for an emergency loan to address unexpected needs that may arise and potentially jeopardize the success of the business. The Wisconsin Women's Business Initiative Corporation incubator in Milwaukee, Wisconsin employs this lending strategy, allowing both men and women to apply for funds with the submission of a business plan, a loan application, and a loan application checklist. The WWBIC's lending program offers loans starting at $1,000.[82] Offering loans in this lower range is important, because these are amounts that would be considered too low for banks to consider lending to applicants while simultaneously being an amount that is too high for applicants who have negative marks on their credit histories to qualify to receive. When WWBIC extends loans, they do so at a significantly lower interest rate than other sources, like the local check cashing businesses, for example, to which entrepreneurs might turn when they are unable to qualify for traditional bank lending to finance their businesses.

Another option for financing that is widely offered by incubators is that of capital referrals. Again utilizing their extensive networks with local banks, venture capitalists and angel investors, incubator managers will assess the financial needs of their residents, help them to assemble a proper loan or capital package presentation, and then connect the client with potential investors in the community that would be best suited for the entrepreneur's purposes. NBIA studies show that 58% of incubators help connect their client companies to investors and strategic partners.

With regular accountability through financial reporting, residents should be able to anticipate most funding needs in advance. If incubator residents anticipate that they will be in need of additional funding to boost their operations, they should contact the incubator manager as soon as the need is anticipated. The incubator manager will provide the resident with an application for funding that will be utilized to direct the manager's search for funding on the resident's behalf. Inevitably, the manager will set up meetings between the incubator resident and prospective funding sources and coach the resident on how to make a presentation to capital providers, from what to say and how to say it to how to put an expert funding presentation process together (this may require the input of a local investor who consults with the incubator). This coaching will continue until the manager has successfully assisted the resident in acquiring the necessary funding. Note that, opposed to a 24-48 hour turnaround that it might take for incubator clients to receive a smaller loan for emergency funds from the incubator, when large amounts of funding are needed, this is often not a quick process. The higher the amount of funds that are needed, the longer the funding process is likely to take.

Technical Assistance

If incubator residents find themselves in need of assistance in a variety of areas offered by the program, they may set an appointment to receive technical assistance. This may come in the form of expert advice and instruction in areas such as marketing, advertising, accounting, goal setting, strategy and planning, law or any other areas in which they lack the knowledge to operate. If incubator staff members are qualified to provide such technical assistance, or if this assistance is not available through incubator staff, volunteer staff should be secured by the incubator manager to provide these services as they are requested. As previously mentioned, technical assistance is ideally offered during the evening hours when the day's activities wind down. All technical assistance hours provided to incubator residents will be logged for statistical purposes.

Value-added Benefits

Incubators of various types offer other value-added benefits to their residents in order to increase the significance of the incubator in the lives of the incubator residents. For example, there may be such benefits as discounts at local office supply stores, free or reduced-price shared software at the incubator, free laptop checkout, free lunch-and-learn seminars held on-site, a free concierge service, negotiated discounts with local hotels, access to an in-house business library, negotiated pick-up and drop off of dry cleaning, childcare discounts, free tickets to local city attractions, reduced tickets to local sporting events to which residents may take their clients, or free use of incubator-owned equipment such as projectors, DVD players, digital cameras, and other items. These value-added benefits come in a number of ways and differ according to the incubator.

Social Responsibility

Because giving back to the community is such an important aspect of being a responsible corporate citizen, incubator managers should encourage their residents to be intentional in giving back to the community. This may take the shape of donating complimentary products and services to schools, community groups and other nonprofits, sponsoring community events, having a presence at events hosted by nonprofits or even serving as speakers for special assemblies and presentations. When incubator clients graduate or spin out of the incubator, this may take the shape of serving as a mentor or providing complimentary or reduced-rate services to other entrepreneurs in the incubator.

Facility Procedures

Incubator developers have a lot invested into their facilities, and as such, they desire to maintain the condition of the incubator. In addition to reviewing facility rules during each new resident's orientation, facility rules should be posted throughout the incubator, and each of the rules should be reinforced as opportunity arises. Violations of facility rules should be immediately addressed in writing by an incubator representative, and a copy of the facility violation should be kept in the resident's file. Another procedural consideration in incubator facilities surrounds cleaning. Ideally, a cleaning service should be contracted to clean common areas on a daily basis, and each incubator resident is responsible for keeping its own office space clean.

Phase 3: Exit Operations

Graduation and "Spinning Out"

Incubators graduate, on average 6.5 companies a year (resident and affiliate client companies combined). In fact, in 2012, business incubators reported having graduated an average of 61 companies from their incubators over the years since opening their doors (resident and affiliate companies combined). [83] To graduate or "spin out" of an incubator simply means to exit the incubator and continue to function as a viable business outside of the incubator space. By the time this season arrives, the business should be stable, sustainable, exhibit steady growth and possess the tools to operate on its own without the incubator's accountability and support. Additionally, when incubated businesses spin out of the facility, they have historically remained in the community or region where they were incubated, contributing to the regional economy as they continue to grow. According to the 2012 State of the Business Incubation Industry report, this trend still continues among incubated businesses throughout North America. When they spin out or graduate from business incubators, 25% of businesses relocate to another space in the same county, 39% relocate to a space in the same city, and 6% relocate to the same neighborhood. Only 13% of incubators reported having graduates that relocated to another county or region in the same state, to another state, or to another country.[84]

According to the most recent industry reports, incubator clients are receiving incubator services for less time before graduating today than in the past. For example, in 2012, industry research showed that incubator residents who received full incubation services graduated within 28 months of being in an incubator program, which is a faster time-to-graduation than reports from only six years prior when incubator clients were graduating within 33 months after receiving full incubation services. Affiliate clients, which typically remain in incubator programs for a shorter time than resident clients, received incubator services for an average of 19 months before graduating, faster than the 23-month time to graduation that was reported in 2006.[85]

The graduation date is usually set or approximated upon the date of the entrepreneur's entry and may be determined by lease expiration or scale. The InBIA classifies graduation triggers into the following categories:

- *Client company spends maximum time allowable in program*
  Some incubators establish the entrepreneur's graduation date (typically one to three years from the date of move-in) much like a traditional lease arrangement, anticipating that with the proper level of engagement in the incubation program, the business should be able to thrive independently by the end of the program.

- *Client company outgrows space available in the incubator*
  In some cases, a company's space needs grow so large that the incubator can no longer house the amount of space that it needs for its operations. In such cases, the company may graduate from the incubator and find a space large enough to house its operations outside of the incubator while still receiving program support from the incubator in most cases.

- *Client company achieves mutually agreed upon milestones*
  Some incubators establish a graduation date according to the business' ability to reach a certain scale or mutually agreed upon milestones. That is, when the business enters the incubator, a plan projecting its financial growth is developed along with milestones that chart its progress according to a specified amount of time. For example, if the incubator projects that the enterprise, with the proper incubation, should hit the $1 million mark in 33 months, the anticipated graduation date is noted on the calendar in 33 months. If the client company succeeds in achieving these milestones in the specified time, it

graduates. If not, the company's projected graduation date is reevaluated.

- *No specific graduation policy*
  There are business incubators that do not have a firm policy for graduation. Instead, they plan for a company's graduation on a case-by-case basis. In some cases, companies are encouraged to remain in the incubator without any anticipated graduation date, most often because they are residents that provide a valuable service to other incubator clients, both those in residence and affiliates.

Of course, graduation timeline adjustments are made by incubator programs as necessary. Some incubator clients significantly exceed expectations and reach their goals much sooner than expected. In these cases, providing the business has been incubated long enough to remain stable, the business spins out of the incubator early (but not prematurely). Further, when they graduate from the incubator, in most cases, the relationship with the program does not end. According to research, 73% of incubators in North America report offering post-incubation services to their incubator clients (as well as pre-incubation services in some cases).[86]

Exit Interview

Because business incubators should be continuously-improving and open organizations that stay on the cutting edge of things, they should always be on the search for feedback that will make their program's organization more effective and more equipped to meet the needs of its incubator clients. It is for this reason that each exiting entrepreneur, just prior to spinning out of the organization, should meet with the incubator's advisory board to share feedback about what was effective and what was ineffective during the incubation process. The exiting entrepreneur should be asked to provide a list of recommendations that will result in the continuous improvement of the incubator so that other businesses can benefit off of the successful entrepreneur's suggestions in the future.

Incubator Alumni

All alumni who graduate or spin out of a business incubator are expected to give back in some way to the incubator program that helped to nurture its growth and development. This may come in the form of mentoring other incubator clients, leveraging connections to assist fellow entrepreneurs with overcoming obstacles, providing complimentary, low-cost or at-cost products and services to incubator clients, or by making financial contributions through the incubator's annual capital campaign. This alumni relationship may be formally established through a signed agreement or as an informal understanding between the incubator and the exiting entrepreneur.

7

The Blueprint

How to Establish an Effective Nonprofit Business Incubator

Now comes the discussion that many would-be business incubator developers have patiently waited for: that of how to actually establish an incubator! Hopefully, reading through the preceding chapters has helped you to establish a comprehensive understanding of the purpose, function, benefits, features, resources and operations of a nonprofit business incubator. In this chapter, we will take a stepwise approach towards assisting you with venturing out to establish your own business incubator.

Prior to beginning this process, we will assume that one the following applies to you:

- You represent a registered nonprofit organization
- You have partnered with a registered nonprofit organization to open the incubator
- You will make the incubator its own registered nonprofit organization

Step 1: Assemble Your Launch Team

Decide on which individuals you would like to work with to plan the development of and establish the incubator. Meet with them, share your passion and enthusiasm with them and sell them on the vision of what you are trying to accomplish. For best results, give them each a copy of this book to aid their understanding of what a real incubator is and does and to inform them about the numerous benefits of business incubation. This team should not be too large. In fact, it is recommended that your team be comprised of no more than five people. Should you desire to incorporate local influencers and community gatekeepers into the planning process in order to leverage their networks or to give them a greater sense of buy-in, maintain your launch team to do the legwork, and place these local influencers on a separate advisory board.

Step 2: Develop a Budget and Seek Funding

Determine how much capital you will need to establish the incubator, and develop a budget based on these projections. Then, decide whether one individual on your team or the entire team will work together on researching and writing various grants and proposals to seek the government funds, corporate sponsorships and private donations necessary to fund the incubator's launch. Then, begin submitting applications and proposals to every potential funding source. Note that fundraising tends to be a lengthy process, and hearing back about the various funding applications and proposals you have submitted may take a while, so begin your fundraising efforts as soon in the planning process (even as early as two years prior to the incubator's projected launch date) as possible.

Step 3: Develop a Business Plan or Feasibility Report

With your team, complete a business plan or feasibility report. Use these research-driven planning exercises to develop a realistic picture of your organization's capacity and readiness to establish a business incubator and to sustain it in the long run. This plan should take an objective look at the funding resources that are available to you, your network of relationships that can be leveraged to make things happen for the incubator, available facilities, staffing resources, and the availability of any other resources necessary to establish the business incubator. After you complete the business plan or feasibility report, have several business professionals review it, and ask them for their feedback.

Step 4: Begin Your Incubator Facility Search

Identifying a facility in which your business incubator can be housed is one of the most critical pieces in the establishment of the business incubator. You should begin your facility search by asking your primary funding source if it owns or has access to any large, empty properties that you can use to house your incubator. If a facility cannot be identified in this way, check with your local city, county or state government about the possibility of purchasing or leasing one of its vacant properties for $1 per year, provided the incubator completes all of the necessary build-out and renovations and that it acknowledges the government agency as a sponsor. Check with local private corporations to inquire about leasing any of their empty, unused buildings or having these spaces donated as their sponsorship of your initiative. If you are unable to secure a facility for your incubator using these methods, work with a local commercial realtor and have him or her inquire about any privately-owned vacant properties in the city that might be available and that fit within your budget. However, before you secure the chosen facility, have the realtor try to negotiate a significantly-reduced rent amount for a long-term lease, and allow this rent reduction to count as the property owner's sponsorship of the business incubator. Finally, when selecting a facility to house your incubator, remember to secure one large enough to accommodate growth.

> *... be intentional about creating buy-in with local community gatekeepers and residents. Nothing can kill a project more quickly than a community that feels imposed upon by a business or organization that moves in without expressing clear consideration for the concerns of those who live in the area!*

Recommendation: If you decide to locate your incubator facility in a residential community, be intentional about fostering a sense of buy-in with local community gatekeepers and residents early in the planning process. Nothing can kill a project more quickly than a community that feels imposed upon by a business or organization that moves in without expressing clear consideration for the concerns of those who live in the area!

Step 5: Build Out and Renovate the Facility

Each incubator facility should offer a variety of workspace sizes and flexible configurations to accommodate their incubator residents' needs, not only considering how the spaces can be used today, but how the spaces can also be easily reconfigured to accommodate their growth tomorrow. During your build-out and renovation process, ensure that you build in a number of individual spaces that can accommodate one to four desks or workstations (remember, if someone comes in as a solopreneur, the goal is to grow the business to multiple employees), small office suites that can accommodate businesses with multiple employees that occupy separate offices within the same space, and spaces for companies that grow within the incubator to employ 20 - 30 people (at a minimum). The goal is for companies to outgrow their initial spaces and move to larger spaces within the incubator as their growth demands, so these larger spaces need to be available.

According to the NBIA, on average, incubators reported utilizing their facility space in the following ways:[87]

- Client companies (54%)
- Common areas (22%)
- Anchor tenants (15%)
- Administrative offices (9%)

Anchor tenants (or residents) are businesses that reside in an incubator facility but do not receive incubation services. They are permitted to lease space inside of the incubator, helping to contribute to the incubator's budget. In addition to serving as a reliable and consistent source of revenue for the incubator, anchor tenants may also support the incubator's program by using some of its leaders to serve as mentors for the start-up entrepreneurs residing in the incubator. In 2012, the NBIA reported that more than half (57%) of incubators in North America had anchor tenants within their facilities. However, incubators should be careful not to fill up their incubator facilities with anchor tenants, recognizing that the majority of the space should be dedicated to housing client companies. The average number of client companies reported by business incubators in 2012 was four.[88]

Other standard spaces to be built into the incubator are:

- Receptionist area
- Conference room
- Training room
- Copy room / mail room
- Break or lunch room
- Equipment storage room
- Restrooms

Depending upon the types of businesses you will house in your incubator, also consider incorporating the following spaces in the facility during your build-out:

- Commercial kitchen (for catering or various food service businesses)
- Inventory/storage rooms
- Large manufacturing / production space
- Garage or loading dock
- Retail store

The build-out of your incubator facility should also include securing (through donations, loans from local your primary funder's inventory, leasing or purchasing) basic office furniture, common area furniture, large and small office equipment, computer technology, networking, building signage, etc. Many incubators will provide these basic operational resources to incubator residents, if at all possible. Any additional furnishings or equipment needs are the responsibility of the incubator resident.

Step 6: Develop a Website

As you begin talking to people in the community about your business incubator, they will naturally want to do a little bit of investigating on their own about your organization. Thus, it is essential that you establish a website. Ensure that your website is professionally designed, attractive to a corporate audience, user-friendly and inclusive of the following:

- The incubator's address, e-mail and telephone number
- The incubator's mission and vision
- The incubator's goals for economic development within the community
- A brief explanation of what business incubation is and its benefits
- Information about the incubator team, including the founding individual(s) or organization, key staffers and advisory board
- Information about what types of businesses should apply for residency
- An application for incubator residency

- Programs and services offered to incubator clients (both resident and virtual)
- A listing of corporate and community sponsors and partners (be sure to keep this part of the website updated)

Step 7: Establish Corporate & Community Partners

Begin spreading the word throughout the community about the incubator that you will soon open and about the great things you plan to accomplish with your business incubation program. Make every attempt to establish official partnerships (and sponsorships) with the local city, county and state governments, prominent community organizations, powerbrokers and gatekeepers in the community, and also with private corporations and individuals who might be interested in assisting with small business development, helping to foster an entrepreneurial climate in their region.

As the incubator build-out and renovation near completion, invite these groups and individuals to see the progress of the project, as this will build their confidence in your incubator organization, add their voices to the base of support for your incubator, and contribute to the buzz about the incubator in the community. Suggestion: Provide all of your prospective partners with a copy of this book so that they, too, might become enthusiastic about business incubation! Remember, most people are unfamiliar with the process of business incubation, so you will need to do a little educating along the way.

Step 8: Assemble an Advisory Board

After you have established partnerships and connections with various corporations, government agencies, community organizations, gatekeepers and influencers throughout the city, decide upon which ones you will invite to become actively involved in your business incubation program by serving on an advisory board, which will provide guidance, direction and support for the incubator organization and its clients. Ensure that you have a broad representation of industries on your advisory board and that you include individuals who function in the following professional positions or possess the following levels of expertise:

- Finance representative
- Investment representative
- Legal representative
- City government representative
- Corporate community representative
- Retail industry representative
- Marketing representative
- Technology representative

Extend to each of the prospective members of the advisory board a formal letter of invitation (which means you should have a logo and letterhead by this time) that includes the following:

- The purpose that the advisory board will serve
- The amount of time that will be required to serve on the advisory board
- The length of the term for the board position
- How frequently meetings are held and their location
- Why the invitee was approached for membership on the advisory board (i.e., because of your expert knowledge in the marketing field, which will add value to our business incubator and its residents)
- What the incubator's expectations will be of the advisory board member (i.e., to help us fulfill our mission of developing businesses by providing guidance, direction and expert advice to the incubator and its residents and leveraging your name and networks to aid them in their entrepreneurial success)

Step 9: Apply for Licenses & Permits

Each city, county and state has different requirements for registering and conducting business, and special rules may also apply for organizations housing multiple businesses. Check with your local and state authorities to ensure that you are in compliance with all regulations and that you will have all of the clearances you need by the time the incubator is ready to open.

Step 10: Begin Creating a Buzz about the Incubator

Essentially, this is your integrated marketing strategy step, which is to begin when your incubator is at least 50% complete and you are able to project a realistic launch date. Send representatives from your launch team out into the community to make presentations to various community groups, business organizations and community events where entrepreneurs gather, informing them about the incubator, the program and services it will offer, and its anticipated launch date. Place materials about the business incubator in plain sight in coffee shops, bookstores and other places that entrepreneurs frequent. Work with local marketing agencies, local businesses and community groups, providing them with polished, professionally-designed marketing collateral (preferably a video) about the business incubator and asking them to blast it to those on their e-mail distribution lists and to post it on their social media pages. Send out press releases with a call for incubator residents to local television news and radio stations. Do whatever it takes to increase the incubator's visibility and generate community conversation about the forthcoming business incubator.

Recommendation: Ask a local public relations expert to donate his or her time to carry out these activities for you in exchange for prominent placement in the incubator's referral directory. When incubator residents are seeking public relations services, this firm will be at the top of the list!

Step 11: Accept Applications for Residency

Once the incubator build-out and renovation are at least 75% complete, begin accepting applications for incubator residency. Each completed incubator residence application should be accompanied by a business plan. If you have created enough of a buzz throughout the community, you can expect to be overwhelmed by the large number of requests for the limited space available in the incubator. At this point, ensure that the screening process is well-defined and ready for execution. This could entail screening by the incubator manager and his or her team, group screenings of the applications by the board of advisors, or a combination of the two. Screeners should produce a list of finalists that will be invited for an interview and for a tour of the incubator space.

Step 12: Invite Finalists for Final Interview and Tour of Facility

By the time finalists are selected and offered an interview, the incubator should be near completion or at least at a point that each of the individual suites and office spaces is built out. Finalists should be given a tour of the incubator facility and the prospective spaces that they would occupy if awarded incubator residency. This tour should occur just prior to the finalist's interview with the screening board. Several interview dates may be necessary if there is an exceptionally-high number of finalists before the final selection of inaugural incubator residents is made.

Step 13: Award Space in the Incubator to Selected Businesses

Formal award letters should be sent to incubator finalists once the final resident selections have been made and spaces have been assigned. Award letters should be followed up with a phone call from incubator staff announcing the entrepreneur's selection as an incubator resident. The award letter should, at the very least, specify the following:

- Notice of being awarded space in the incubator
- The amount of space being offered to the business in the incubator (square footage, number of offices)
- The amount of rent that the resident will pay and when the first payment is due
- The term of the lease in the incubator
- The first date available for move-in into the incubator
- The new resident's orientation date

- A request for the business to formally accept or decline residence in the incubator and sign the lease by a certain date

Step 14: Establish an Incubator Policy & Procedures Manual

This is a step that can begin as soon as the final plans for the incubator are set in place and can proceed simultaneously as the other steps are being executed. The incubator manager and staff should work together to create a comprehensive manual that contains all of the incubator's official policies and procedures, as well as the disciplinary actions and consequences surrounding their violation. When beginning this project, I recommend that you do not reinvent the wheel. Instead, search the internet for an existing policy and procedures manual that has already been published online by another incubator or business development organization and request permission from the proper contact to adapt the manual for your own use (if such permission is required). A copy of the official Policy & Procedures Manual should be disseminated to all incubator residents during their orientation, and an agreement stating that they have received, read, understand and agree to abide by its contents should be signed and placed in their resident file.

Step 15: Establish a Lean Staff / Technical Assistance Team

Begin hiring considerations for incubator staff early. Many times, the first place that incubator developers will look when seeking to hire a staff is their launch team, individuals who have been working incessantly to plan, establish and promote the incubator prior to its opening, because these individuals tend to be passionate about the incubator and its mission. However, it is not a given that those who are instrumental in helping to establish and launch the business incubator will be a great fit for working on the incubator staff. Hiring for an incubator staff necessarily includes targeting individuals with a passion for business development and who possess expert-level technical skills that will be of value to incubator residents. Each staff member should be able to provide direction and guidance in *at least* two major areas of technical assistance in order to be a good fit for the incubator, especially considering that the size of the initial staff will be quite small in many cases.

For the areas of technical assistance not covered by paid incubator staff members, begin making contacts with local experts that will donate their time to providing a certain number of on-site technical assistance hours to incubator clients, at least on a weekly basis. Should additional services be required of these technical assistance providers beyond that of the guidance and direction they can offer to incubator clients free of charge, the incubator manager should negotiate a reduced rate with them at which incubator residents may individually contract their services.

Step 16: Develop and Present an Incubator Resident Orientation

The first cohort of business owners to be awarded residence in the incubator should attend orientation together to create a sense of camaraderie and community. During this orientation, which ideally should be led by the incubator manager, residents will receive a copy of the incubator's official Policies & Procedures manual, and they should view a presentation that includes explanations of the following:

- What to expect in and from the business incubator
- Incubator hours of operation, after-hours policies, and access procedures
- Incubator security procedures
- Shared office equipment policies and procedures (any copy codes or other access codes should be disseminated at orientation)
- Incubator resident expectations (trainings, continuing education, monthly meetings, reporting, etc.)
- Where and to whom residents should go to receive various services offered by the incubator
- Information about custodial services and policies for office cleanliness and upkeep of common areas
- Maintenance request procedures

- Incubator visitor policy (signing incubator guests in and out)
- Parking policies
- Incubator's policy concerning pets in the office
- Graduation or "spinning out" policy

Step 17: Wrap Up the Final Details

At this point, all of the major work in preparation for the incubator launch should be completed, and all that should remain are the final details. The incubator staff should assist with these tasks, which include but are not limited to:

- Generating all necessary administrative forms needed for incubator residents and placing them in a centralized area (in the facility or online) for easy access
- Inventorying all of the incubator's office equipment, technology, software, etc.
- Posting instructions, policies and procedures throughout the facility as necessary
- Posting attractive directional signage throughout the facility
- Purchasing office supplies, such as replacement ink and toner cartridges, print and copy paper, etc.
- Ordering operational supplies such as restroom and break room paper goods

Step 18: Plan an Incubator Launch Reception for Key Influencers & Local Media

Once the hard launch date for the incubator has been established, have invitations professionally designed and mailed and/or emailed to various key corporate, political and professional influencers in the community with an invitation to attend the formal launch reception. This invitation list should include but not be limited to:

- City, county, state and federal government representatives
- Presidents of local chapters of national business and professional organizations in the community

- Key influencers in the corporate community
- University representatives (high-ranking officials)
- Business development organization leaders
- CEO's, presidents and vice presidents of prominent businesses in the community
- Banking and finance executives
- Venture capitalists, SBDC leaders, and angel investor fund representatives
- Local newspaper, television, radio and social media representatives

Prior to this launch reception, resident businesses should have sufficiently moved into their spaces, and there should be attractive signage outside of their spaces signaling their identity and what they do. As guests walk throughout the launch reception (preferably enjoying music, refreshments, drinks, etc.), they should have the opportunity to interact with incubator residents and staff, speak with members of the board of advisors (who should be well-versed on the mission and operations of the incubator) and gather literature about how to sponsor, partner with or donate funds, products and/or services to the incubator organization.

Recommendation: After this initial exposure to the incubator and its residents, information about the incubator will spread like wildfire throughout the community, and other influencers will also want to experience the incubator by taking their own tours. Always be prepared to give a tour to these individuals, and ensure that the tour guide is well-versed on the mission, vision and operations of the incubator. If staffing does not allow for tours on demand, post incubator tour hours on the website and on the doors of the incubator, offering them at several set times each week during the first few months of the incubator's opening, and less frequently after the incubator has been open for some time.

Step 19: Plan an Open House for the Surrounding Community

In order to bring individuals in the surrounding community aboard as partners, be intentional about inviting them into your incubator for an open house just for them. Doing so will increase their level of buy-in and increase support for your incubator program and mission. The format of the open house should be basically the same as the launch reception for the key influencers, and it should be advertised in advance through local vehicles of communication (social media, local organizations, posting at local stores and coffee shops, etc.) in order to provide ample time for planning to attend.

Step 20: Cut the Ribbon and Open for Business (Make It a Media Opportunity!)

On the official launch date, invite the local mayor, members of the local city and county government, important community representatives, business VIPs and corporate sponsors for a ribbon cutting ceremony in front of the incubator. Be sure to invite as many media representatives as possible, as this is a significant occasion that will command key media coverage. Allow a few elected officials and key sponsors to have words of congratulations and support at the podium, ensure that you have an opportunity to address the audience from the podium to clearly re-state the incubator's mission and goals, cut the ribbon, and open the doors for business!

8

The "Controversy" Chapter

Innovating the Process of Business Incubation

Innovation is the true mark of entrepreneurship in its purest sense, and I find an individual's ability to innovate a product or concept irresistibly interesting. You know, the kind of innovation that comes out of nowhere leaving you scratching your temple and asking, *How did they come up with that? Why didn't I think of that? Why hasn't anyone else thought of that before?* My hat goes off to anyone who has the ability to innovate anything, because it is, to me, one of the boldest and most dynamic expressions of brilliance and creativity! Innovation demonstrates a person's ability to take the limits off of his or her imagination and see beyond what is seen and commonly accepted as the standard or the norm. Additionally, such innovation is a visible display of their mental genius as they tap into intellectual processes that others have not tapped into in order to produce what others have not thought to produce. Simply put, innovators take what already exists, reconfigure it or destroy and rebuild it differently, and produce something new. I love, admire and applaud innovation in its every form!

That said, I would not be true to myself if I did not make an attempt to innovate the universally-accepted, traditional focus of business incubation in the U.S. Until this point, our focus has been about building an effective business incubator that focuses on developing start-up and early-stage businesses that can survive and thrive on their own. The emphasis of this focus is to do whatever it takes to increase the business's revenue so that it can generate greater profit, hire more employees, grow larger in scope and contribute to the local economy and entrepreneurial climate. To incubate a business to this level requires careful, intentional focus on the business itself with close accountability to meeting strategic goals, financial projections and all of the other good textbook tools and processes that come along with establishing a profitable business. The goal: incubate businesses and make them grow as quickly as possible!

However, allow me to throw a wrench into this concept, just for your consideration. I call this chapter the "Controversy" Chapter because there are two innovations that I would like to introduce to challenge the traditional focus of business incubation, and each of the two innovations requires a primary focus on incubating something other than the start-up or early-stage business itself. These innovations might be considered by some to be controversial because they represent a departure from the norm. However, both of these innovative approaches are inspired by pioneers in business incubation, entrepreneurship and organization, and if embraced by business incubator developers, could potentially increase levels of effectiveness in building thriving start-ups in our communities. It is my hope that each of these innovations will stimulate you to the point that you begin to think out of the box when constructing your own business incubator!

Incubation Innovation 1:

*Rather than focusing on incubating the *business*, focus on incubating the *entrepreneur*.*

Inspired by Della Clark,
President of The Enterprise Center, West Philadelphia, PA

As previously mentioned, Della Clark, President of The Enterprise Center (formerly the West Philadelphia Enterprise Center) in West Philadelphia, PA, has been leading a business incubation program that has been upheld as a model business incubator for decades. In addition to winning the InBIA's Incubator of the Year award, The Enterprise Center also has an award-winning youth entrepreneurship program, and a Magic Johnson / HP Digital Inventor Center, among other impressive offerings. The incubator itself is a beautiful sight to see, and its core initiatives are quite impressive. However, what is even more impressive is the success rate of the entrepreneurs that come through the incubator's program. At The Enterprise Center, business stars are made, and many entrepreneurs from around the nation would do anything for a coveted spot at The Enterprise Center's table.

One critical practice of this highly-effective incubator program is that the incubator focuses primarily on developing the entrepreneur rather than the business that he or she owns. Clark holds the belief that if you focus on developing the entrepreneur, you will not have to worry about the business; if the entrepreneur is successful, so will the business be successful. This will most likely be a revolutionary idea to many in the small business development industry, perhaps even a controversial one for many incubator managers, but one cannot deny The Enterprise Center's phenomenal success in operating with such a focus. Clark is not afraid of going against the grain and doing things differently. She clearly explained the mindset behind her innovative approach towards incubation during an interview:

Quite frankly, we don't focus on the business here. I would probably best describe it as this: we're in the talent business. We look for talent, because it matters not the business. ...Let's say, for instance, I've got talent that is selling parts to the airplane industry, but the University of Pennsylvania calls me up and has got a million dollars in mulch business – as in, they're looking for somebody to sell the University a million dollars worth of mulch. If I've got somebody that has talent, they recognize a good opportunity. They don't say, 'Well, I'm not in the mulch business, so I'm not going after that business.' Right? What we try to do here is produce talent. Talent, then, recognizes opportunity. And if the opportunity makes sense, then they develop a business around that opportunity. If you focus on the business all the time, that business is a very narrow vision.

Clark promotes focusing on developing the entrepreneur more so than focusing on the development of the business, and while the approach itself may be an unconventional departure from business incubation norms, The Enterprise Center has birthed many millionaire businesses utilizing this approach. The logic behind the approach is two-fold. First, when the incubator successfully develops the entrepreneur, if the current start-up business fails, the entrepreneur will still possess the mentality, skill sets and tools – the business-building talent – necessary to bounce back and apply this talent to the development of a new enterprise. If, on the other hand, the incubator's focus is on incubating the start-up, and the start-up idea fails, the entrepreneur (whose talent has not been fully developed because the incubator's focus was intently on developing and growing the business) may not possess the business-building talent to identify and pursue other opportunities for success; thus his or her entrepreneurial journey ends with the closing of the current start-up business.

Second, if an incubator primarily focuses on developing the entrepreneur rather than the start-up, the entrepreneur will possess the flexibility to seamlessly move from one industry to another and from offering one product or service to another. Because the entrepreneur possesses highly-developed entrepreneurial proficiencies, this business-building talent can be successfully translated to any entrepreneurial opportunity. Thus, with this innovation, the incubation emphasis is not about the start-up company that an entrepreneur is running, but it is about the entrepreneur who is running the company.

Incubation Innovation 2:

Rather than focusing on incubating the *business*, focus on incubating an awesome organization.

Inspired by Katherine Catlin and Jana Matthews, authors of Building the Awesome Organization, published by Kauffman Center for Entrepreneurial Leadership[89]

Catlin and Matthews co-authored a wonderfully-written book with a mission: that of helping entrepreneurial leaders build awesome organizations that achieve entrepreneurial growth. Based on their work, the innovation to traditional business incubation that I would like to offer to incubator developers is this: rather than focus your development on building start-up businesses, focus your development on building highly-effective, or awesome, start-up business *organizations*. If you focus on developing highly-effective business organizations rather than on simply trying to develop the business itself to make it profit and grow, the business will, by default, grow, thrive, and become profitable (because highly-effective organizations result in environments that make things grow)! Again, this could be considered a controversial notion in the business incubation industry, but it all depends on how you choose to view it. What is considered controversial to some is considered innovative to others!

The premise behind Catlin and Matthews' work is that very few entrepreneurs recognize the critical importance of building awesome organizations, and as a result, few succeed in doing so. Most entrepreneurs, by necessity, focus on the nuts and bolts of building, production and delivery of their products and services, but they do not place intentional focus on building effective organizations, which is necessary for their continued growth and sustainability. Thus, it is the incubator's role and responsibility to help them to do so, not only so that the start-ups can grow today but so they can survive in the long term and continue to see tomorrow.

Catlin and Matthews offer a number of characteristics of awesome organizations, which I assert that innovative incubator managers should focus on developing in their client companies.[90] How can incubators know if they are developing highly-effective, awesome organizations among their incubator clients? When incubators have effectively focused their efforts on developing awesome start-up organizations, they will observe the following characteristics present in their client companies, for example:

- They will have a shared vision and core values that everyone understands and embraces.

- They will have a culture that rewards people for their ideas and contributions and fosters great teamwork at all levels.

- They will have people who are dedicated to learning and helping others learn.

- They will anticipate change and continually redefine every part of the business to ensure that its competitive edge is always sharp and distinctive.

These characteristics represent only a sampling of Catlin and Matthews' characteristics that describe an awesome organization, and these characteristics are scarcely seen in a typical small business. So often, small business owners are so busy about the work of staying afloat, managing crises, making payroll and putting out fires that they become consumed with the day-to-day activities of running the business. Thus, if they become successful, they become successful in building a *business* – not an awesome and effective *organization*.

You are likely wondering, *Why is building an awesome organization even necessary*? The easy answer for this is that building an organization is critical if the business is going to succeed in the long term, because an awesome organization possesses the structure, culture and resources that are needed to successfully overcome roadblocks, navigate obstacles, adjust with market shifts, manage conflicts, and handle any other challenges that could threaten a business' ability to survive and thrive. Without building a highly-effective organization, an entrepreneur is essentially leaving his or her business' ability to overcome such challenges to chance, thus threatening its ability to survive long term. Yes, entrepreneurs can build a growing business, but it will eventually falter if they do not build an awesome organization.

Consider this perspective from an entrepreneurial expert featured in Catlin and Matthews' research:

Typically a business doesn't move in a straight line; there are lots of turns in the road, lots of unexpected obstacles that you come up against. It's the awesome organization that can navigate around those obstacles to reach success. In a lot of early-stage companies, leaders spend all their time on building the product and then when you get internal conflicts or changes in the market, you spiral down and lose momentum because you haven't built the organization.[91]

If an entrepreneur does not consciously, intentionally build an awesome organization, an organization will haphazardly form all by itself – and anything that is haphazardly formed will be a far cry from what one would build on his or her own with intentional effort. I call this haphazardly-formed organization that emerges by default the "accidental organization." Whether you incubate one or not, an organization *will* develop around your business activities. In this accidental organization, employees will operate out of a set of core values, but are they the start-up founder's desired core values or each individual's own subjective set of core values? There is a company culture present, but is it a positive one that intentionally fosters camaraderie, teamwork, sharing and trust, or one that thrives on strength of personality, negativity, criticism and individualism that develops accidentally on its own?

Unless incubators are intentional about helping their clients to develop awesome organizations, including a desired culture, processes, adaptability, ability to execute, ability to envision and plan for the future, and willingness to work as a team, their clients, by default, will allow accidental organizations to emerge that will fight against the business growth into which they have invested a great part of their time, energy and resources. Catlin and Matthews advise:

Adrenaline can get your first product out the doors, but if you're going to build a multi-product company, you need organizational tools and processes to surmount the complexity. A few years down the road, adrenaline just doesn't do it anymore. Having these organizational tools and processes in place enables the company to keep working on existing products while senior management focuses on the future.[92]

In their initial stages of growth, start-ups can get things done and even experience growth and profitability without a lot of organizational intentionality, structure or effort; things are simple, and the processes necessary to function are very basic ones. However, as the company grows and becomes increasingly more complex, greater levels of organizational structure and controls are needed in order to manage the growth and maintain the company's effectiveness. This is the point, often occurring later down the road, at which most companies begin to look at their organizations rather than just their businesses. The drawback is this: they have operated within the context of an accidental organization for so long that bad habits, a counterproductive culture, and poor processes have developed and become the norm among their workers. Now, rather than starting the building of an effective organization from scratch, they are faced with the difficult task of getting their team to unlearn the poor habits that developed during the formation of the accidental organization and implement the new healthier habits, culture, and processes that are necessary for the company to grow, survive and thrive long term. For best results, incubators should focus their efforts on helping their start-ups develop highly-effective, awesome organizations from day one.

There is another reason that incubators should consider primarily focusing on developing awesome organizations rather than simply start-ups. When an incubator can successfully develop awesome organizations, if a start-up falters and has to shift its product, service or industry focus, or even if it has to shut down operations and start a brand new business, its employees are more prone to stick with the organization! Employees value working with an awesome organization, so they will desire to remain a cohesive unit, working on whatever product or service the organization offers. They love working together as a team, they love the atmosphere and creativity, they love the mutual support, and they love the chemistry and atmosphere. They will stick with the organization, even if it means that they will initially receive less compensation, work longer hours and be challenged to attack a new industry learning curve that is a mile high. People remain committed to awesome organizations, not to mere businesses. People will go through the *fire* with an awesome organization, but they will easily jump ship when things start to get a little too warm for a mere business!

If you, as an incubator developer, can incubate awesome organizations, which are the carefully-constructed frameworks or contexts into which businesses can grow and survive long term, you can incubate any business inside of them! Simply put, if you incubate the organization, the business will grow. Why sink loads of cash, time and energy into a business that, when it finally reaches a desired level of complexity or hits a big wall, will be unable to survive because its infrastructure and organization are shaky? Build intentional awesome organizations block by block, and they will be able to withstand any growth challenge!

For those who have managed to buy into this incubation innovation, Catlin and Matthews' Six Components of an Awesome Organization, are essentially the building blocks, excluding none, that must be "consciously built and continuously strengthened if you want your company to grow."93

Catlin & Matthews' Characteristics of an Awesome Organization

Culture for Growth

An empowering, motivating environment that attracts awesome people and then retains them because it enables them to thrive and perform at their best.

Awesome People

The know-how, skills, insight, imagination and ideas of your people are the intangible assets that give your company its distinct competitive edge.

Plan for Growth

A written, yet flexible, plan that defines the long and short-term requirements for growth and innovation, which helps guide decision making and enables everyone to focus on projects, tasks and activities that lead to achievement of the vision and goals.

Top Team as Leaders of Growth

Because the CEO cannot do it alone, each member of the top team needs to share the vision and fully understand his or her functional and cross-functional roles and responsibilities for implementing the plan and achieving the mission.

Infrastructure for Growth

The infrastructure comprised of finding and leading people, planning and alignment, and management and control that enables you to institutionalize the organization's mission, vision and values and makes the work flow easily and efficiently.

You, the Awesome Leader of Growth

As the company grows, your ability to communicate a powerful sense of purpose and direction will help align everyone with the mission, vision and values, and this will be one of the keys to your success.

If these components threaten to be a bit challenging to you as an incubator developer, or even as an entrepreneur, you are not alone. The authors explain:

Very few entrepreneurs have mastered all six components. Some entrepreneurs know they have to hire great people, but they don't know how to create a culture that will help them retain these people. Some know they have to do a better job with planning, but they don't develop the infrastructure that enables plans to be implemented. Others hire and fire top team members without knowing how to build a cohesive top team, what roles team members need to play, and how their own role will change as the team matures and/or the company moves into a new stage of development.[94]

Catlin and Matthews' *Building the Awesome Organization* is a must-read for incubator managers who are willing to adopt this innovative approach, focusing their business incubation efforts on developing awesome organizations rather than merely good businesses. They utilize research from some of the top CEOs in the U.S. to teach, in detail, entrepreneur leaders and developers how to accomplish each of the Six Components of an Awesome Organization through a plethora of ideas, exercises, survey tools, surveys and reflection questions.

❖

In this chapter, I have sought to present two business incubation program innovations for your consideration, not necessarily for the purpose of changing your mind about how to construct your incubator, but to prime the pump of innovative thinking pertaining to incubating start-up and early-stage businesses. If you desire to lead an effective business incubator that accomplishes its mission of nurturing and growing businesses to the stage of viability, you *must* be an innovative thinker. Your incubator clients are depending on you!

As the chief problem-solver for your incubator clients, in order to effectively assist them with achieving their enterprise goals, it is a requirement that you be able to think out of the box, entertaining any and all possibilities that will lead to helping your clients with overcoming their obstacles and attaining their goals. Sometimes, the traditional route works, and sometimes it doesn't. Sometimes, creativity and innovation – going against the grain, breaking all the rules, and tossing the textbook out of the window – can be your best friend. In any case, I encourage you to step out of the box, be willing to explore the world of business incubation, add your own innovations as you go along, and share them with your peers in the incubation industry so we can succeed together in our collective mission of nurturing successful entrepreneurs.

Happy incubating!

NOTES

[1] Knopp, L. (2012). *State of the business incubation industry*. Athens, OH: NBIA Publications.

[2] International Business Innovation Association (2017). Retrieved from http://www.caled.org/nbia-is-now-inbia-the-international-business-innovation-association/

[3] National Business Incubation Association. (2010). Retrieved from http://www.ukspa.org.uk/members/nbia

[4] Scott, W. (1998*). Organizations: Rational, natural, and open systems (4th ed.).* Upper Saddle River, NJ: Prentice Hall.

[5] Parsons, T. (1960). *Structure and Process in Modern Societies*. Glencoe, IL: Free Press.

[6] Scott, W. (1998*). Organizations: Rational, natural, and open systems (4th ed.).* Upper Saddle River, NJ: Prentice Hall.

[7] IBID.

[8] Arrow, K. (1974). *The limits of organization*. New York: Norton. (p. 68)

[9] Knopp, L. (2007). *State of the business incubation industry*. Athens, Ohio: NBIA Publications.

[10] IBID.

[11] IBID

[12] IBID.

[13] National Business Incubation Association website. (2010).

[14] Clark, D. & Minor, T. (2000). *Business incubators: A formula for minority business success*. Retrieved from www.tmaonline.net/Business_center/Articles/incubator.htm

[15] National Business Incubation Association website. (2010).

[16] Knopp, L. (2012). *State of the business incubation industry*. Athens, OH: NBIA Publications.

[17] Knopp, L. (2001). International conference examines business incubators as tools for accelerating economic growth. Retrieved from www.nbia.org/resource_center/in_the_news/nbia_press_releases/05072001_2.php

[18] National Business Incubation Association website. (2010).

[19] Greene, P. & Butler, J. (1996). The minority community as a natural business incubator. *Journal of Business Research*, 36, 51-58.

[20] Gibbons, T. (2002). *Incubators give big hand to small businesses*. Retrieved from www.cgi.jacksonville.com/cgi-bin

[21] Campbell, C. (1989). Change agents in the new economy: Business incubators and economic development. *Economic Development Review*, 7, 56-59.

[22] America's Small Business Development Centers. Retrieved from http://americassbdc.org/about-us/history/

[23] Campbell, M. (2001). *A happy ending: Incubators offer nurturing environment*

for small businesses. Retrieved from
www.more.abcnews.go.com/sections/business/YourBusiness/smallbizbuilder010
613. html

[24] Knopp, L. (2012). *State of the business incubation industry.* Athens, OH: NBIA
Publications.

[25] Garrity, C. (2002). Incubators can get your company off ground. *The
Birmingham Business Journal.* Retrieved from:
Birmingham.bizjournals.com/Birmingham/stories/200/08/19/focus2.html

[26] Putnam, F. (2002). Bessemer's two incubators nature start-ups. *The
Birmingham Business Journal.* Retrieved from:
Birmingham.bizjournals.com/Birmingham/stories/2002/10/28/focus2.html

[27] Gerber, M. (2003). *The E-Myth revisited: Why most small businesses don't work
and what to do about it.* New York: Harper Collins.

[28] National Business Incubation Association website. (2010). Retrieved from
http://www.ukspa.org.uk/members/nbia

[29] Rubin, T., Aas, T., & Stead, A. (2015). Knowledge flow in technological business
incubators: Evidence from Australia and Israel. *Technovation.* 41–42, 11–
24. doi:10.1016/j.technovation.2015.03.002

[30] Knopp, L. (2012). State of the business incubation industry. Athens, OH: NBIA
Publications.

[31] CPAC. (1998). *New study shows business incubation has significant economic
impact.* Retrieved from www.cpac.missouri.edu/newsuse/archive/981209

[32] Knopp, L. (2012). *State of the business incubation industry.* Athens, OH: NBIA
Publications.

[33] IBID.

[34] Allen, D. & McCluskey, R. (1990). Structure, policy, services and performance in
the business incubator industry. *Entrepreneurship Theory and Practice,* 14
(Winter), 61-77.

[35] Knopp, L. (2012). *State of the business incubation industry.* Athens, OH: NBIA
Publications.

[36] IBID.

[37] IBID.

[38] Allen, D. & McCluskey, R. (1990). Structure, policy, services and performance in
the business incubator industry. *Entrepreneurship Theory and Practice,* 14
(Winter), 61-77.

[39] Knopp, L. (2012). State of the business incubation industry. Athens, OH: NBIA
Publications.

[40] Knopp, L. (2007). *State of the business incubation industry.* Athens, OH: NBIA
Publications.

[41] Wisconsin Women's Business Initiative Corporation, wwbic.com

[42] National Business Incubation Association website. (2010).

[43] National Business Incubation Association website. (2010).

[44] Erlewine, M. (2007). Comparing Stats on Firm Survival. In *Measuring Your
Business Incubator's Economic Impact: A Toolkit.* Athens, Ohio: National Business

Incubation Association.

[45] Garrity, C. (2002). Incubators can get your company off ground. *The Birmingham Business Journal*. Retrieved from: Birmingham.bizjournals.com/Birmingham/stories/200/08/19/focus2.html

[46] NBIA. (1990). The State of the Business Incubation Industry, p. 11-13.

[47] Spitzer, Jr., D. & Ford, R. (1989). Business incubators: Do we really understand them? *Frontiers of Entrepreneurship Research*. Wellesley, MA: Babson College. P. 436-446.

[48] Businessdictionary.com/definition/synergy.html

[49] Jumpstarting Business Ventures. 2002. Lesson 17: Business incubators. Retrieved from www.jbv.com/lessons/lesson17

[50] Sherman, H. & Chappell, D. 1998. Methodological challenges in evaluating incubator outcomes. *Economic Development Quarterly*. Retrieved from www.dotcomventuresatl.com/incubenews014.htm

[51] Garrity, C. (2002). Incubators can get your company off ground. *The Birmingham Business Journal*. Retrieved from: Birmingham.bizjournals.com/Birmingham/stories/200/08/19/focus2.html

[52] Knopp, L. (2012). *State of the business incubation industry*. Athens, OH: NBIA Publications.

[53] Gibbons, T. (2002). *Incubators give big hand to small businesses*. Retrieved from www.cgi.jacksonville.com/cgi-bin

[54] IBID.

[55] Knopp, L. (2012). *State of the business incubation industry*. Athens, OH: NBIA Publications.

[56] Knopp, L. (2012). *State of the business incubation industry*. Athens, OH: NBIA Publications.

[57] Knopp, L. (2012). *State of the business incubation industry*. Athens, OH: NBIA Publications.

[58] Burger, F. (1999). Business incubators: How successful are they? Area Development Online. Retrieved from www.area-development.com/past/jan99/features/incuba.htm

[59] Campbell, M. (2001). *A happy ending: Incubators offer nurturing environment for small businesses*. Retrieved from www.more.abcnews.go.com/sections/business/YourBusiness/smallbizbuilder010613. html

[60] Greene, P. & Butler, J. (1996). The minority community as a natural business incubator. *Journal of Business Research*, 36, 51-58.

[61] Darwin, J. (2002). New incubator to cater to ex-Enron employees. *Houston Business Journal*. Retrieved from www.houston.bizjournals.com/Houston/stories/2002/01/21newscolunn4.html

[62] IBID.

[63] CPAC. (1998). *New study shows business incubation has significant economic impact*. Retrieved from www.cpac.missouri.edu/newsuse/archive/981209

[64] Campbell, M. (2001). *A happy ending: Incubators offer nurturing environment*

for small businesses. Retrieved from
www.more.abcnews.go.com/sections/business/YourBusiness/smallbizbuilder010
613. html
[65] Jumpstarting Business Ventures. 2002. Lesson 17: Business incubators.
Retrieved from www.jbv.com/lessons/lesson17
[66] Kearns, M. (2000). *Business incubators hatch home-grown jobs.*
www.nbia.org/resource_center/in_the_news/nbia_press_releases/010000.php
[67] IBID.
[68] Knopp, L. (2012). *State of the business incubation industry*. Athens, OH: NBIA
Publications.
[69] Molnar, L. & Gilette, L. 1996. *Sustaining economic growth: The positive impact
of the Michigan incubator industry 1985-1995.* East Lansing: University of
Michigan Business School and the Michigan Business Incubator Association.
[70] Jumpstarting Business Ventures. 2002. Lesson 17: Business incubators.
Retrieved from www.jbv.com/lessons/lesson17
[71] Knopp, L. (2012). *State of the business incubation industry*. Athens, OH: NBIA
Publications.
[72] NBIA, 2002.
[73] Knopp, L. (2012). *State of the business incubation industry*. Athens, OH: NBIA
Publications.
[74] Knopp, L. (2012). *State of the business incubation industry*. Athens, OH: NBIA
Publications.
[75] Gibbons, T. (2002). *Incubators give big hand to small businesses*. Retrieved
from www.cgi.jacksonville.com/cgi-bin
[76] National Business Incubation Association website. (2010).
[77] Garrity, C. (2002). Incubators can get your company off ground. *The
Birmingham Business Journal*. Retrieved from:
Birmingham.bizjournals.com/Birmingham/stories/200/08/19/focus2.html
[78] Smilor, R., Gibson, D. & Kozmetzsky, G. (1988). Creating the technolopolis:
High-technology development in Austin, Texas. *Journal of Business Venturing*, 4,
49-67.
[79] Rice, M. & Abetti, P. (1992). *Intervention mechanisms utilized by business
incubators to influence the critical success factors of new venture: An exploratory
study.* Paper presented at Babson College Entrepreneurship Conference, INSEAD,
Fontainbleau, France.
[80] Greene, P. & Butler, J. (1996). The minority community as a natural business
incubator. *Journal of Business Research*, 36, 51-58.
[81] CHDC. 1998. Strategic framework for commercial revitalization.
http://policy.rutgers.edu/cupr/community/organizations/projcomm/wsp/revite1
3.html
[82] Wisconsin Women's Business Initiative Corportion. (2017). Retrieved from
https://www.wwbic.com/finance-your-business/faq---wwbic-loans/
[83] Knopp, L. (2012). *State of the business incubation industry*. Athens, OH: NBIA
Publications.

[84] IBID.

[85] IBID.

[86] IBID.

[87] IBID.

[88] IBID.

[89] Catlin, K. & Matthews, J., Kauffman Center for Entrepreneurial Leadership. (2002). *Building the awesome organization: Six essential components that drive entrepreneurial growth*. Kansas City, MO: Kauffman Center for Entrepreneurial Leadership, Ewing Marion Kauffman Foundation.

[90] IBID.

[91] IBID, p. 1.

[92] IBID, p. 4.

[93] IBID, p. 7.

[94] IBID.

About Shannon Cormier Williams, Ph.D.

Dr. Shannon Williams, a native Houstonian, is an entrepreneurial evangelist, writer, researcher and consultant. Her research examines the intersections between entrepreneurship and economic development, specifically how incubating micro-enterprises in disadvantaged communities can result in the socioeconomic transformation of these emerging markets. Dr. Williams is the founder and co-founder of successful businesses that have beaten the odds to survive and thrive for more than a decade. As an entrepreneurship lecturer in Atlanta, Georgia, she enjoys teaching and transferring her passion for entrepreneurship to young university students. As a consultant, she advises community and economic development groups, training them on how to establish business incubators that effectively nurture entrepreneurs in the creation of sustainable enterprises that build strong communities.

.

Printed in Great Britain
by Amazon

46493953R00102